Law Enforcement Education
in the Middle Grades:
Police/Student Relations

Law Enforcement Education in the Middle Grades: Police/Student Relations

By Phyllis P. McDonald

The Curriculum Series

Produced in cooperation with
the National Association
of School Counselors

National Education Association
Washington, D.C.

Copyright © 1978
National Education Association of the United States

Stock No. 1710-2-00 (paper)

Note
The opinions expressed in this publication should not be con-
strued as representing the policy or position of the National
Education Association. Materials published as part of the NEA
Curriculum Series are intended to be discussion documents for
teachers who are concerned with specialized interests of the
profession.

Library of Congress Cataloging in Publication Data

McDonald, Phyllis P.
  Law enforcement education in the middle grades.

  (The Curriculum series)
  Bibliography: p.
  1. Law enforcement—Study and teaching. 2. Juvenile delinquency—Prevention. 3. Public relations—Police. 4. Police
services for juvenile. I. Title. II. Series.
HV 7923.M23   364'.07'12   78-17863 81- 4271
ISBN 0-8106-1710-2-00 pbk.

CONTENTS

PREFACE

The police element of the criminal justice system captures the attention of the young mind far more quickly than any other element because the function of the law enforcement officer brings excitement, intrigue, sirens, mystery, red lights, and gory crime scenes. While court, corrections, parole, and probation personnel come into play as an aftermath, their functions are quite mundane compared to the curiosity generated by brass buttons, a hip-holstered .38, and a gold badge.

The information provided in this publication will serve not only the teacher or police officer who wishes to replicate the instructional program in his/her jurisdiction; it also will provide a point of departure for the teacher or police officer whose interest and imagination leads to extended classroom discussion in areas relevant to the age in which we live. To induce learning about a vocation which is continually in the news and which is the subject of fictional stories and nightly television entertainment will indeed dispel myths concerning the police function and will give a greater appreciation for the role of the keeper of the peace. While every question asked by a student is not always answered within the content of the subject matter, often the teachers' guides have partial answers or at least some discussion that leads to a logical response.

Because of the value of good police/student relations, I have fully supported this instructional program since its inception. I know of no other such effort combining the talents of the academic community with those of active police officers to produce a course of study so vital to a youngster's developing years.

COLONEL KENNETH W. WATKINS
Superintendent of Police (Retired)
Montgomery County, Maryland

The Author
Dr. Phyllis P. McDonald was Director of the Police/School Delinquency Prevention Project for Montgomery County (Maryland) Public Schools as well as Program Manager for the Model In-Service Training Program, Montgomery County (Maryland) Department of Police.

Consultant
The following educator has reviewed the manuscript and provided helpful comments and suggestions: Andrew M. Poston, social studies teacher, Washington Junior High School, Nashville, Tennessee.

INTRODUCTION

The Police/Student Relations Program (PSR) was conducted pursuant to a grant from the Governor's Commission on Law Enforcement and the Administration of Justice for the State of Maryland (Law Enforcement Assistance, Administration, U.S. Department of Justice) under the Omnibus Crime Control and Safe Streets Act of 1968, Grant No. 5109-POL-6. The project was under the direction of the author who was then with the Montgomery County Public Schools in cooperation with the Montgomery County Department of Police.

The problem addressed by Police/Student Relations is one which is becoming increasingly serious and which is receiving more and more attention by national leaders. The magnitude of the problem of juvenile delinquency is more serious not only because of increasing proportions of youth committing crimes but also because of changes in the nature of the crimes. Offenses are occurring among younger youth and inside schools as well as outside schools. Serious offenses (murder, rape, arson, assault, burglary, etc.) committed by persons under eighteen are increasing. In Montgomery County, Maryland, the number of such offenses by persons under eighteen increased by 16 percent over a four-year period. Further, the myth that poverty is a primary causative agent for delinquency is being exploded in the seventies as serious delinquency spreads to all income levels.

Delinquency prevention programs in the United States have been largely hit-or-miss affairs—projects with little reliable evaluation, small in magnitude, and scattered geographically. Many programs which were successful on a small scale have raised doubts in the minds of persons who wished to duplicate them because of questionable evaluation techniques and special characteristics of the population served which might have affected the results.

Several approaches have been tried. The nature of the programs has been dependent, for the most part, upon the implementing agency and the type of design. Programs providing one-to-one counseling services have been the most popular since the 1930's. This type of program makes the assumption that the cause of delinquency is the delinquent. Other sociologically-oriented programs have expanded to family counseling, big-brother programs, and walk-in counseling or recreation centers seeking to repair a damaged juvenile or family. While some have appealed to healthy parts of the human system, none has taken advantage of the logical processes which are an important aspect of psychological functioning.

Although many community agencies, including police departments, have attempted programs to quell the rising tide of delinquency, seldom has the school been utilized to its fullest advantage. Even less frequently have schools and police departments worked together. Many police programs tried in schools have been patterned after the psychologically oriented one-to-one counseling approach.

A recent report by the National Association of Counties identified the following key elements in delinquency prevention:

1. Once an adolescent becomes involved in the juvenile justice system, the likelihood of his/her becoming a recidivist increases.
2. Prevention programs which provide youth an opportunity to interact with adult models are more effective than programs which ultimately label individuals as delinquent by virtue of the fact that adolescents are involved in a special program.*

The Police/Student Relations project, an innovative, proven, effective, prevention program, is a totally new approach to delinquency prevention. When you read the program description, you will recognize parts of familiar program plans. The uniqueness of the PSR approach, however, is that these familiar pieces have been fashioned into a new and successful type of program. The Police/Student Relations project is not a pill or a bandage to be applied to repair; rather it is a program to enhance and to take advantage of certain natural abilities and characteristics which allow children to continue functioning in a

---

* Aurora Gallagher, ed., *Juvenile Delinquency: A Basic Manual for County Officials* (Washington, D.C.: National Association of Counties Research Foundation, Criminal Justice Program, 1976).

healthy way. It seeks to stimulate the logical thought processes of students so as to bring about attitude change — not through brainwashing, values clarification techniques, or cajoling, but through the delivery of a direct, adult message which provides students with information upon which to base decisions about individual behavior. Police/Student Relations attempts to impact adolescents *before* they make decisions which ultimately involve them in the juvenile justice system.

The PSR program concept conveys the message that each person is responsible for her/his own behavior; but, more critically, that each student is fully capable of receiving information about an adult system and processing that information in a responsible manner.

Police/Student Relations is delivered to all students; the program does not isolate, identify, and label a group of students who may be regarded as predelinquent or potentially delinquent. The teacher in PSR sets the stage for a highly reputable adult model to interact with students: the police officer.

CHAPTER 1
A DESCRIPTION OF THE
POLICE/STUDENT RELATIONS
(PSR) PROGRAM

BACKGROUND

Juvenile delinquency can be considered an antisocial act, a means to fulfill personal consumer needs, a personal pathological plea for attention, or a way of life. Whatever the motivation, the law enforcement profession must devote excessive amounts of time processing juveniles as delinquency increases at an alarming rate. Since social institutions other than the criminal justice system help to create the problems, these institutions have the potential for developing effective prevention programs.

Montgomery County, Maryland, was designated the most affluent county in the United States in 1973.[1] Despite its affluence, however, the increase in juvenile delinquency kept abreast of the national rate. The increase nationwide for 1973 was from 10 percent to 35 percent.[2] Montgomery County juvenile arrests increased 25 percent in 1973 and again in 1974.[3] These figures should not be surprising. Hirschi refutes the claim that juvenile offenders are largely from poverty areas: "There appears to be little or no relation between the socioeconomic status of an area and its rate of self-reported delinquency. The percentages reporting one or more delinquent acts by school range from 36 percent in Portola, the junior high school highest in socioeconomic status, to 49 percent in El Cerrito, the senior high school highest in socioeconomic status."[4] Programs in delinquency prevention, therefore, should be conducted across youth populations in all socioeconomic strata.

The major social institutions with the potential to develop broad prevention programs to combat delinquent acts are the police and the schools. These two institutions deal with the same populations of youth; they represent authority to juveniles; they should therefore present a united, consistent front to young people. Flammang believes that the school is "one of the most effective and cooperative juvenile resources within the community. Its role in the total police juvenile enterprise cannot be overstated." [5]

ATTITUDE AND BEHAVIOR CHANGE

Attitude and behavior change which results in reducing the number of juvenile offenses is one goal of prevention programs. The critical time for attitude change in the development of the person is "during the period of middle childhood through early adolescence" (grades 6–12).[6] Furthermore, at this critical period of development the school is in a position to exert a strong influence. When the adolescent asserts his/her independence by rejection of the views of his/her parents and other adults, the school has an opportunity to become a positive force in attitude development.

The goal of the cooperative Police/Student Relations project (PSR) is to influence the attitudes of adolescents toward law enforcement officers and subsequently to influence the behavior of these young people. The law enforcement curriculum which is planned to be taught in junior high school seeks to change adolescent behavior by—

1. Providing students with an opportunity to interact with police officers in a nonadversary setting which allows them to see officers as living, breathing human beings rather than as television fantasies put on the street to harass adolescents. This positive interaction is important. The police officer is the new visible symbol of authority with whom increased contact is anticipated for the teenager. Generally, the aggression of young children is expressed and contained within the home. During the teen years, however, aggressive acts are more likely to spread to and be committed within the community, entailing confrontation with a police officer.

2. Providing students with accurate, in-depth information as to how the officer actually performs his/her job—e.g., students are instructed to run a polygraph machine, to protect a crime scene, to conduct a concentric circle search, and to lift latent fingerprints from glass bottles, just as recruits at a police training academy are taught. Such instruction provides a needed alternative to the TV image of a police officer.

THE ROLE OF THE TEACHER

The program is administered primarily by the school system instead of by the police department. The classroom teacher carries the burden of instruction in that he/she has the major responsibilities to structure the class, to plan and select student activities, to acquire and distribute materials. The police officer enters the classroom after the instructional process is under way and as a support or supplement to the ongoing instruction. The program is, therefore, economically feasible for the department of police.

The instructional and audiovisual materials have been prepared. Teachers (and police officers) need not spend time researching the subject area, designing classroom activities, locating appropriate audiovisual materials, or preparing worksheets or assessment tasks. The result is that teachers are more willing to teach the subject of law enforcement. As a matter of fact, the reaction of some teachers is eagerness to teach the subject because of the quality (as well as the completeness) of the instructional materials which are designed to offer maximum flexibility to teachers. Neither the units nor the performance objectives are hierarchical or sequential; therefore teachers can select topics for instruction on the basis of the needs, interests, and learning characteristics of their students.

THE ROLE OF THE POLICE OFFICER

The police officer makes guest appearances in the classroom when requested by the teacher for clarification of technical materials, questioning by students, and relevant discussions.

The officer is a part of the ongoing instructional process rather than a one-time lecturer; his/her appearances are therefore more meaningful. The teacher introduces students to the vocabulary and mechanical principles of the polygraph, for example. When the officer arrives, he/she can proceed to other aspects and applications of the subject in greater detail.

THE COURSE

The course in law enforcement for junior high school students is a curriculum innovation in Montgomery County. In order for this innovation to be successful, teacher and student instructional materials must be offered along with the curriculum guide. As Lawler states, "A feature of the current curricular innovation developed by national committees is the special pupil-and-teacher-materials prepared for each of the programs, including not only texts, but also film, film-strips, slides and kinescopes. It appears that we have at last learned that if curricular innovations are to become institutionalized, student materials appropriate for the innovation must be provided." [7] Thus, the units developed include all audiovisual materials, guides, and instructional worksheets.

The course, entitled *Law Enforcement and Crime Detection,* consists of nine units. Seven of the units can be offered to any junior high school class; two are more appropriate for ninth grade.

Unit 1, Careers in Law Enforcement, has a dual purpose. It seeks to change student attitudes by allowing students to gain some understanding of the personal problems inherent in the law enforcement profession—fear of injury, high standards for performance demanded by citizens. In addition, it acquaints students with the entrance standards, training, and continuous monitoring of behavior experienced by law enforcement personnel.

Unit 2 is the first of three units in **Criminal Investigation** and focuses on **Evidence.** Precision, accuracy, and care in handling evidence are emphasized in order to prepare well for trial.

Unit 3 consists of **Criminal Investigation, Specific Crimes.** Here students gain an appreciation of the number of different approaches to criminal investigation. They have an opportunity to explore investigation of arson, homicide, truck hijacking, narcotics, burglary, robbery and larceny.

Unit 4, Criminal Investigation, Suspects, explores issues related to processing suspects. Procedures include interrogation, interviewing, polygraph, voicegraph, and lineup. In each case the admissibility or inadmissibility of evidence in court is examined.

Unit 5, Investigation of Juveniles, is approached from the point of view of the police officer rather than from that of the rights of the student. Most of the information, however, should be useful to students. Options available to runaways and cases of child abuse are considered. Arrest procedures and circumstances determining whether a case goes to adult court or to juvenile court are presented in a step-by-step sequence.

Unit 6, Patrol, gives students an opportunity to role-play many of the situations with which a patrol officer copes in his/her daily job.

Units 7 and 8 deal with **Forensic Science.** They are appropriate for ninth grade science classes since most of the material consists of actual laboratory procedures used to analyze physical evidence.

Unit 9, Issues in Law Enforcement, is the last in the series. Here students explore contemporary issues or problems, particularly those which may lead to changes in law enforcement (e.g., women in law enforcement; height, weight, and age requirements; capital punishment; the role of the victim; crime prevention programs).

Outlines which list performance objectives with matching content, strategies, resources, and assessment tasks are available for each unit. Bonus materials include vocabulary exercises, extended activities, a book of police slang, jokes, and culminating activities.

The design of the curriculum and materials permits great teacher flexibility in program planning. Activities for each day of instruction may be chosen depending on student needs and interests. A sample weekly plan for **Unit 2** on **Criminal Investigation: Evidence** might consist of the following:

Day 1

Audiovisual slide tape on physical evidence. Students, in small groups, survey a school area to identify physical evidence.

Transparency on types of searches. Small groups of students directed by other students conduct specific types of searches and critique each other.

Day 2

Transparency on protecting the crime scene. Students are given role cards, among them that of the first officer to the scene who must decide which of the others should be admitted to the crime scene.

Day 3

Videotape on homicide. Students view mock homicide and compare perceptions as to what took place, followed by a discussion of problems with eyewitness accounts.

Videotape on homicide. Students view videotape, set up mock crime scene, sketch crime scene, and make decisions as to measurements to be included on sketches and types of photos to be taken.

Day 4

Filmloop on how to lift latent fingerprints. Students practice lifting fingerprints from different surfaces. (If possible an officer attends class.)

Day 5

Filmloop on how to record inked fingerprints. Students practice recording and classifying inked fingerprints of each other. (If possible an officer attends class.)

ADDITIONAL INFORMATION

WHEN STUDENTS ASK . . .

1. *What will I get out of this course?*

   You will learn about law enforcement—mainly how and why the police work as they do (here in Montgomery County). When police officers visit the class, you will be able to ask them questions about their lives and their work. I hope that one thing you will gain from this course is a feeling that law enforcement is understandable, that the whole system is more comprehensible for you.

2. *How will this course affect my future?*

   It will give you a small experience of what law enforcement is like so that you can decide whether you would like to seek a career in the field. It will make you aware of career possibilities in law enforcement at local, state, and federal levels—working for a public agency or for a private company. You will learn about a range of jobs and the different skills, abilities, education, and training which they require. No matter what your own aptitude, you will probably see a realistic career opportunity for yourself if you decide that you are interested in the field of law enforcement.

3. *What will we do in the course?*

   You will participate in activities designed to give you an opportunity to do what a police officer would do. For example, you might learn the communications code, how to lift and classify fingerprints, or what to do first when you arrive at the scene of a crime. You will have experience in looking at a situation involving law enforcement with an investigator's or a police officer's responsibility predominantly in mind.

4. *How will this course help me to understand current events better?*

   You will see how the efforts of the police serve the administration of justice—in other words, how the work of the police fits in with the work of the courts, the work of the legislature, and with corrections programs and facilities.

5. *Will I have a chance to learn about how law enforcement affects me and my friends?*

   Yes, in Unit 5, you will get a chance to examine the special character and goals of the juvenile justice system, including procedures for juvenile arrests, prosecution, treatment, and aftercare.

6. *What will be expected of me?*

   You will be expected to participate in classroom activities. In addition, in interacting with police officers who come to class as resources for learning, you will have a chance to broaden the officers' knowledge of and experience with students—in a learning situation where neither of you is seen as a villain.

7. *What are the PSR materials like, anyway?*

   The materials are NOT—

   a. A philosophic essay on "Why We Need Laws in Society."
   b. Information which would help students know how to be a better criminal (or to become a criminal).
   c. A set of rules for legal behavior—like the Ten Commandments.
   d. A crash course in ethical philosophy which invites endless armchair discussion on the nature of good and evil in the world.

e. A list of homilies and platitudes.

f. A compendium of the disasters which befall wayward youth.

g. A program to make overly legal-minded junior lawyers out of students.

h. An anarchist scheme to focus on student rights as the first step in overthrowing the established public school system.

i. A fascist scheme to focus on unquestioning obedience and the virtues of orderliness and discipline.

j. A list of suggestions for teachers to spend hours gathering materials, reading books, and preparing lesson plans.

k. A set of lists and descriptions of duties and procedures and organization charts and chains of command for students to "sit quietly at their desks and study."

l. A way to get police officers into schools to pursue undercover activities.

The materials *ARE*—

a. Units which show students how the law is enforced (in Montgomery County).

b. Activities which provide students with experiences in acting "like a police officer" in solving crimes.

c. Content packages in a variety of forms which give students information and which dispel myths and fantasies about the criminal justice system and the juvenile justice system.

d. Specific tasks which show and/or allow students to experience a little of what it is like to be a police officer.

e. An attempt to reduce delinquent behavior.

f. An attempt to improve student attitudes toward authority figures in general and toward police in particular.

g. An effort to expose students to career options and possibilities in the law enforcement field.

h. A hands-on approach where students actually *do* some of the things police officers would do in carrying out their work.

i. Complete instructional packages which include lesson plans, student activities, and worksheets with accompanying instructions and answers, audiovisual materials, lists of additional resources and where to get them, and teachers' guides which contain background information and answers to questions frequently asked by students.

A COMPARISON OF POLICE/STUDENT RELATIONS TO SIMILAR PROGRAMS

Table 1 at the end of this chapter is a review of other police/school programs. The advantages and disadvantages listed are generalizations which pertain to the program classification but not necessarily to the program cited as an example.

Among all such programs, the Cincinnati Police Juvenile Attitude Project is most similar to the Police/Student Relations Project in concept and in operation. Both are curriculum development models but with certain critical differences which are outlined in Table 2.

Three elements appear to make Police/Student Relations successful: the educational features, the involvement of police officers in ongoing classroom activities, and the consistently positive attitude change of students involved in the program.

Table 1
Taxonomy of Police/School Delinquency Prevention Programs

Type of Intervention Strategy	Example of Program	Advantages	Disadvantages
Law-Related Education: Students receive information about laws, court system, and its functions	Carroll County, Maryland	Structuring a K-12 program; each grade has topic to cover — no overlap or duplication	Few materials — teachers must prepare their own program, time-consuming, no quality control
	Georgetown Street Law Project, Georgetown University, Washington, D.C.	Materials focus on legal situation student or citizen may face	Information generally too abstract for junior high school students; no back-up materials, just curriculum guides
	Cincinnati, Ohio	*Six*-week program changed attitudes significantly	Approach is to try to directly convince students to follow rules
Randomly Selected Police: Random classes; rap sessions	Alexandria, Virginia	Different officer assigned to schools each week for presentation	Instruction generally limited to one or two sessions with officer — no continuity; each session different
Random Classes: Assigned officer(s); rap sessions	Bismarck, North Dakota Chesapeake, Virginia	Same officers providing instruction become familiar with students and pertinent issues; excellent for small school system	Not economically feasible for police department serving large school district
Selected Officers	Long Beach, California	Instruction authentic — presented by officers	Not economically feasible for police department serving large school district; generally officers do not have back-up materials
Police serve students involved in juvenile justice system, i.e., counseling	Dallas, Texas Alexandria, Virginia Flint, Michigan	Students involved in minor offenses or status offenses diverted from juvenile justice system.	Not preventive approach
Teachers provide instruction in law enforcement, schedule officers for highly technical topics, all back-up materials provided	Montgomery County, Maryland, Police/ Student Relations	Economically feasible for police serving large school district.	Quality of instruction may vary to some extent from teacher to teacher

Table 2
Comparison of Police/Student Relations Project to Cincinnati Police Juvenile Attitude Project

	PSR	Cincinnati Project
Scope of Evaluation	Attitude tests Content tests Comparison of arrest statistics to determine if behavior change accompanied attitude change	Attitude tests only
Attitude Test Results (Grade 7)	Length of time compared (two, four, nine weeks) — statistically significant attitude change all time periods Two weeks of instruction — statistically significant favorable attitude change	All tests combined (two or six weeks of instruction) — no attitude change Two weeks of instruction — worsening of attitude
Arrest Statistics Results	Pre- and post-offense rates — statistically significant lower rate after instruction	None
Content Test Results	Pre- and post-instruction — significant learning occurred in experimental group	None
Underlying Psychological Approach	Curriculum presents objective technical information about job of law enforcement officer; student infers that authority administered professionally and can be fair and just and is necessary for welfare of society Psychological dynamic: Adult provides objective information; student treated as adult capable of receiving and processing information and forming values and judgments	Curriculum delivers indirect moralistic, judgmental message — rules are good and necessary Psychological dynamic: Parent message places student in child role implying student needs to be "told," not capable of thinking for self; not "safe" for student to draw own conclusions
Underlying Educational Approach	Students continuously engaged in learning skills of crime detection to build appreciation for law enforcement as legitimate profession with technical skills (e.g., students lift latent fingerprints, record and classify inked fingerprints; learn radio communications code and other criminal investigation and patrol skills)	Students active participants in traditional classroom learning activities, but passive recipients of information in interesting, real-world subject areas (e.g., teacher lectures, students given written assignments)
Flexibility	Units and days not sequential or hierarchical; teacher has flexibility, can select materials to match interests and needs of students; units can be used in any junior high school year Curriculum horizontal design — content learning activities, audiovisual resources, and assessment tasks developed for each performance objective (teacher can choose topic for each day and also specific performance objective(s))	Curriculum designed to be taught in sequence over three-year period; materials hierarchical (some topics repeated each year, more in depth)
Teacher Preparation	All instructional materials provided (teacher's guides, content handouts, audiovisual resources, student worksheets and other materials, assessment tasks for performance objectives) No teacher research necessary	Curriculum outline and limited number of student materials provided; audiovisuals suggested but most are general, commercial productions Teachers must do research to acquire some necessary materials

CHAPTER 2
WHY DOES THE PSR PROGRAM
WORK WHERE SO MANY
OTHERS HAVE FAILED?

Any instructional program sets psychological and behavioral processes into motion. The design of the PSR program impacts in several ways on the internal thought processes of students. The results are evident in the behavior change, reflected by the offense rate, of the students.

This chapter is based on observations about the PSR program, good sense about program impact, and some knowledge of the internal processes which change people's attitudes and behavior.

PROCESSES WITHIN THE STUDENT

There is a certain psychology inherent in the design of the PSR law enforcement instructional materials which communicates a special message to students, and thus alters the teacher-student dynamic in the classroom. Instruction is presented in the objective adult mode, i.e., the ego state described in the Transactional Analysis theory of behavior. The mode of instruction appeals to the adult ego state of the student. In most instructional programs designed to improve relations between police and students or to reduce juvenile offenses, instruction is couched in the "parent" mode and results in "hooking the child" in the student. Often the learner resents the inherent message, feels as if he/she is being preached to, or has the sensation that someone is trying to manipulate instead of level with him/her. Junior high school students are particularly sensitive to having moral judgments, values, and preachments of parents imposed upon them. The adolescent in the junior high school years is at a turning point in his/her personality formation, feeling pressure to separate his/her identity from that of his/her parents and to seek a unique identity. At this time he/she has a low tolerance for "you should" or "you should not." The PSR instructional program provides students with objective information and expects them to formulate judgments by inference from the information supplied. For example, the materials never say, "Police officers are nice guys, and you should like and appreciate them." Instead the nature of the instruction demonstrates that the officer must perform his/her job with precision and accuracy (e.g., the collection of physical evidence must be precise and scientific to enable the prosecution to win the court case). Students, standing in the officer's shoes, perform these same functions and build an appreciation for the law enforcement profession rather than for the "niceness" of an officer.

Further, learners have an opportunity to observe the teacher and the police officer working cooperatively in their approach to students. This approach of two authority figures displaying consistent behavior helps to clarify the role of authority in society for adolescents.

All students receive the PSR instruction. The program does not seek out, identify, and highlight those who are already delinquent or judged to be predelinquent. Programs which are designed to treat delinquents, which isolate them and consequently label them as different from their peers, are ineffective in combatting delinquency. Thus, alternative schools and programs, court-prescribed counseling and probation are not effective deterrents. The fact that such programs may appear to the child to preserve his/her preciousness as a delinquent may serve to reinforce and enhance delinquent behavior.

An additional benefit of the PSR program is the in-depth exposure to an occupation which helps to move the adolescent toward a career choice. This important process can promote sound mental health through integration of the ego and can result in fewer antisocial acts.

PROCESSES BETWEEN THE STUDENT AND
THE POLICE OFFICER

The fact that the law enforcement profession, which is generally closed to laypersons and most especially to youth, is willing to allow students to enter its world by sharing precise techniques and procedures with them is an edifying experience for youth. Further, the shared information provides a link between students—often isolated in schools—and the real world. Young people, with natural survival instincts, perform better when presented with an authentic part of the world which they will enter as adults.

The instructional process in the subject of law enforcement is started by the classroom teacher. This situation allows the officer to enter the classroom in an edified role. After students have learned some of the language and rudiments of law enforcement, the police officer arrives to provide more technical knowledge. At this point students and police officer can begin their relationship on a common ground with the common language and bond of law enforcement between them. The discussion is at a more sophisticated and meaningful level than the typical one-lecture police visit which tends to remain at the level of the dramatic experiences of the officer. Further, the relationship based on a mutual interest tends to continue outside of the classroom, in the shopping centers, and on the street, with the result that police/student relationships on the street are less strained and volatile. Instead of directing expletives at an officer on the street to gain peer admiration and approval, the student can ask about fingerprints or other areas of police work discussed in class. He/she can engage in new behaviors and interact positively with an authority figure.

As the student learns about the officer's job, she/he can begin to identify with the officer and with the fears and problems of the job as well as with its satisfactions. The student begins to know what the job "feels" like by role-playing—making decisions, performing tasks similar to those of the officer. Experience and knowledge of the training, skills, and technical accuracy required help the student develop a new appreciation for the job and for the person of the officer. Unrealistic aspects of the media image of law enforcement personnel are also counteracted. The individual officer appears in a different light—as a person distinct from the institution of which she/he is a representative.

New intellectual and emotional insights enable the student to reassess and/or modify his/her attitude and behavior concerning law enforcement at home, in school, and in the community. He/she can also begin to consider and appreciate a career in law enforcement.

An additional benefit of the PSR approach is borne out by recent research which found that programs which make adults available to youth interacting in a vocational capacity to provide a model are more effective delinquency deterrents than adults treating adolescents (i.e., in counseling situations).[1]

BENEFITS FOR THE STUDENT

One of the unexpected side effects of the course was discovered: The student who learns the "ins and outs" of law enforcement makes more effective personal decisions. The course offers information on many problems which face teenagers—running away, shoplifting, felonies versus misdemeanors, and subsequent consequences. When given all the data on these various problem areas—consequences, treatment possibilities, alternatives—the student can make a more informed decision. "Is running away best? If so, how can it be done safely?" "Will shoplifting a $10 item lead to a permanent record?" "What's the difference in consequences of going to adult court instead of juvenile court?"

Students are not always aware of the exact role of the police officer and ascribe powers to her/him that she/he does not possess. "The police officer sets the fine for the traffic violation." "He/she places those stop signs at inconvenient places." "He/she only arrests people when he/she feels like it." "He/she could tell the judge to let you go if he/she wanted to."

Certain units in the course are designed to help students understand the role of the police in the criminal justice system. The regular police officer cannot set fines, alter a judge or jury's decision. (Actually, in court cases the officer is often in a very humble position: she/he presents the evidence in as accurate a manner as possible, and the remainder of the case proceeds without his/her intervention.)

After exposure to the PSR program, students will hopefully emerge with a more realistic view—no longer blaming the officer on the street for all their woes—and with an understanding of the limits of police powers.

Too often students see the officer as an enemy and do not make the connection that police science is a possible job or career field. This course helps them make the connection. **Unit I** in *Law Enforcement and Crime Detection* is concerned with **Careers.** Students who begin to consider a career in law enforcement start to relate differently to the officer on the street. They begin to gather information about jobs: How tall do you have to be? Are there any females in the department of police? Do candidates have to know how to shoot, or will the police department train them? The positive identity with police which begins to form shapes the nature of the interaction between the student and the officer.

BENEFITS FOR THE TEACHER AND THE POLICE OFFICER

In the class situation students are not the only persons affected by the instructional process. The teacher may come away with a different attitude and a new respect toward officers: "They're human." "They treat each student who asks a question as though he/she were the most important person in the world. I'm going to try and treat my students like that in the future."

Teachers' attitudes are frequently affected through the instructional process. Teachers are exposed to the information and become involved in performing many of the learning tasks with the children. In addition, they enjoy the same opportunity as their students in interacting with the police officer. It should not be assumed that all adults have positive attitudes toward law enforcement or an appreciation for the law enforcement function in society. Teachers' attitudes were formed in the same way as the attitudes of the adolescents in their classrooms— by on-the-street experience (sometimes negative), media portrayals, and peer influence.

Similarly, the police officer is changed after the experience. He/she enters the classroom expecting to have to be entertaining and tell war stories. Instead she/he finds a group of adolescents who speak her/his language and can discuss issues in law enforcement. The fact that a student has taken the time to become acquainted with the job and the problems it entails is flattering to even the most crusty officer. Further, students may ask technical questions of officers on the street. The reaction on the part of the officer is sometimes clearly shock. One veteran officer confronted the PSR coordinator within the police department and demanded to know how a student had information about lifting latent fingerprints sufficient to ask him (the officer) a question on the street. After the program was explained, he grudgingly admitted that perhaps the program was a good idea.

In summary, the instructional process changes the dynamics between the officer and the student and between the officer and the teacher. A further question now remains to be investigated: Does the instructional program or process also change student attitudes toward authority figures generally? If so, how and why, and to what extent?

PROCESSES BETWEEN THE STUDENT AND SOCIETY

AN UNDERSTANDING OF LAW ENFORCEMENT IN SOCIETY

In a student's mind, and sometimes in the adult mind as well, the "institution" of law enforcement is intertwined with and is the same as the personality and behavior of the law enforcement officer. Personal experiences or peer values may serve as the basis of an attitude toward the officer and may be applied equally toward law enforcement as an institution.

The PSR course in law enforcement is designed to separate in the student's mind the institution of law enforcement in society from the police officer—the person. The student learns the basics about law enforcement from the classroom teacher and from media productions. Subsequently, the officer visits the classroom for technical presentations. At this time, the student can interact with the officer and can experience different personalities and approaches. The differentiation of the institution from the individual representative of that institution is important in the formulation of attitudes toward the structure of society. More importantly, the student begins to consider the decision-making process used to select persons to become officers and the system used to control their behavior. With this important information she/he can begin to think more clearly about where and in what sectors of society change may be needed.

The concept of differentiating an institution from some of the persons who represent it can be applied to school, government, social service agencies, and religion.

The student, consistently put in the role of the police officer or investigator throughout the course of instruction, begins to identify with the officer's function in society. Identification with authority reduces antisocial behavior aimed at combatting or being disrespectful toward authority.

As students learn about the subject and function of law enforcement in society separate from the police officer, they begin to develop an appreciation for the role of law enforcement in society separate and distinct from the personality of the police officer. In other words, there is an opportunity to formulate ideas and opinions about law enforcement independent of whether or not the officer in the classroom or on the street has been courteous or harrassing to a particular student. Further, at the same time the officer enters the classroom, downstream of the instructional process, learners can accept the individual officer as a human being with personality characteristics which do not necessarily speak for the law enforcement process.

The fact that the teacher presents the basic information and then involves the police officer in the instructional process allows students to form attitudes toward law enforcement as a function in society. They, then, interrelate with the officer and begin to differentiate between their attitudes toward law enforcement and their liking or disliking of the personality of the individual officer.

POLICE, TEACHERS, PARENTS! THEY'RE ALL AUTHORITY FIGURES!

Perhaps of far greater importance than currently recognized is the united working front presented by two of the most important authority figures in a student's life, the teacher and the police officer. Some teachers may believe that to establish their credibility with students, they must attack the institutions with which students sometimes appear to be in conflict. The police officer represents one of those institutions. The two professionals working together present a different message: that the learner will no longer be successful in pitting one authority against another. This same phenomenon occurs in the family when parents are not in agreement in their approach to disciplining a child. Often the child subconsciously senses the division and attempts to further divide the parents, to the supposed advantage of the child.

By the time the student reaches junior high school, many of his/her problems are expressed outside the home and on the street. As a visible symbol, the police officer is the authority figure who will most often have to deal with antisocial adolescent behavior. The school experiences its share of such behavior as well. If a student begins to view police officers positively and attempts to develop constructive relationships with them, then there is a good chance that some of that positive view will be transferred to other authority figures —i.e., to parents, teachers, and principals.

ELIMINATION OF FANTASIES GENERATED BY THE MASS MEDIA

The PSR program helps to eliminate many fantasies generated by the mass media. Many students do not know what happens to a juvenile when she/he is arrested. They speculate, "You're beaten," "You're photographed with a number across your chest," "You're thrown in a jail cell to wait two months for trial." For some, "Nothing happens. The guy gives you an ice cream cone, pats your hand, and says, 'Don't do it again!' " For others the reality is more severe than the fantasy, particularly when, unexpectedly, the parents are involved very early in the juvenile justice process. Still others discover they can stop defending themselves so stringently against "the cops" who aren't rude tough guys after all, but most of whom are fairly objective, just doing a job.

APPRECIATION FOR PROFESSIONAL PREPARATION

The course in law enforcement is highly technical in some areas and encourages an appreciation for professional preparation. Precision and accuracy are emphasized. A technical level of knowledge is generally synonymous with a concrete level of operation. Sometimes concrete presentations are more stimulating, particularly to junior high level students. Further, the average student is more likely to become involved with the information. As a result, learners develop an appreciation for the amount of exact, scientific knowledge acquired and used by the well-trained officer. Overall, students begin to understand the need for specialized knowledge, the concept of preparation and training, and their relationship to professionalism.

PROCESSES BETWEEN THE STUDENT AND THE INSTRUCTIONAL PROCESS

The instructional and audiovisual materials of the PSR program are designed to actively involve the student in thinking processes. Students are always more interested in learning when they can become personally involved. Many activities require them to solve problems and make decisions just as an officer would have to do on the job. For example, students are shown three to four slides of a fire scene and then are asked to make a decision as to whether or not the evidence suggests arson.

The learning activities are skill-oriented. Students learn how to perform procedures by actually doing them instead of passively reading about them. For example, learners have an opportunity to conduct three major types of search: concentric circle, point to point, and sector. They lift latent fingerprints, record and classify inked fingerprints, sketch and photograph (using polaroid) a mock crime set up in the classroom.

The instruction is not hierarchical. Within each unit are five days of instruction with performance objectives for each day. The days can be moved around in order of presentation or can be selected to meet the needs of teachers and/or students. Teachers who prefer may select only one performance objective on any given day and instruct within those limits. This approach is possible since an audiovisual resource, strategies, content, and assessment tasks are available for each performance objective. The instructional materials have been designed for several styles of teaching. If whole group instruction is preferred, the teacher's guide should be followed. Each guide has several strategies to accompany the audiovisual resource. Strategies may be chosen on the basis of need or enjoyment. If individualized instruction is preferred (for the entire class or for only a few students with special needs), a learning center may be set up using the audiovisual material and the worksheets which are designed to be self-instructional. Answers are included on the worksheets to allow students to check their work. (If you are fearful that students will fill in the answers and thus "cheat" a little, remember that research has shown that with self-instructional materials students learn just as much by copying the answers.)

OTHER CHARACTERISTICS OF THE INSTRUCTIONAL MATERIALS

POORLY MOTIVATED STUDENTS

The PSR course was developed originally as a high-interest course for students experiencing severe problems in school. It is considered suitable for those who are poorly motivated or who are not experiencing success in the regular academic curriculum. During the pilot sessions instructors noted that fewer behavior problems were exhibited while students were in the law enforcement class.

CRITICAL THINKING SKILLS

Critical thinking skills have been incorporated into both the instructional materials and the audiovisual materials. Performance objectives are based on content, verbs which describe a higher order of thinking skills, and a type of learning activity appropriate to the content. Table 1 on page 36 lists verbs used to develop performance objectives. For example, the format for the slide/tape *Fire Investigator* is designed to reinforce the skill of inferential thinking. The point to be gained from the topic is that a fire scene can be examined for evidence of arson. The slide/tape is designed so that students are presented first with slides depicting evidence, then are asked to decide whether or not the evidence would lead the investigator to suspect arson.

Other types of thinking skills incorporated into the audio-visual and instructional materials include:

• problem-solving
• brainstorming, divergent thinking
• prioritizing, alternative or consequences search
• decision-making, deductive thinking
• application of principles or generalizations to specifics
• concept formation

GRADING

These units can be graded and integrated into the curriculum in several ways.

Option 1. If law enforcement is taught as part of a social studies course (Youth and the Law or Urban Studies), regular letter grades can be assigned for however many weeks the course is taught based on the quality of performance or the results of periodic or final examinations.

Option 2. All units are self-correcting for the student. At the top of each worksheet (which the student can choose to complete or not) a space is provided for the learner to note the number of items completed. "Completed" means the item was attempted, and the response was checked against the correct answer. If the response is incorrect, the student is directed to fill in the correct answer.

A form is available for the learner to record the number of performance objectives he/she completed for the total number of units in which instruction was received. Grades can be assigned, if needed, on the basis of the number of performance objectives completed. This system of grading, known as the continuous performance evaluation, is based on the principle that one should not be labeled a "failure" if the real problem is that one cannot learn as rapidly as another learner. The teacher can allow the student as much time as required to recycle her/his work until she/he is satisfied with the amount that has been completed.

Option 3. The teacher can contract with students for better grades individually or as a group. The criterion is set for each grade, e.g., 16 performance objectives plus 3 extended activities per unit earn the grade of A. Students state prior to the beginning of instruction which grade they will contract for, and they should be held to the agreement.

Option 4. A system of instruction to assess students on the basis of whether or not each has achieved competency is more difficult to establish. The PSR materials have been designed to make this system a semi-reality for the classroom teacher by providing an assessment task for each performance objective. A criterion (i.e., the number of correct responses one must achieve to be considered competent) has been established for each assessment task. In the event a student does not achieve competency, she/he would be allowed to do additional work in that performance objective learning area and recycle.

The basic principle behind this approach is that each learner can achieve a prescribed level of competency, although it may take one longer than another. This system obviates a student being labeled a "failure" because his/her learning rate is different from that of another. One either achieves competency or one does not. One may interpret one's behavior as "failing," but the decision has been one's own and one must live with it.

Table 1

Suggested Verbs for Writing Performance Objectives and Assessment Measures*

Knowledge	define, recognize, describe, select, recall, identify, name, list, state, match, point out
Comprehension	translate, interpret, relate, categorize, classify, infer, generalize, predict, explain, outline, paraphrase, restate
Application	apply, solve, relate, prove, test, diagnose, develop, compare, select, plan, design, explain, defend, choose, justify, predict, determine, construct
Analysis	distinguish, identify, detect, relate, conclude, determine, diagram, infer, analyze, compare, describe, interpret, critique, explain
Synthesis	design, produce, conduct, combine, recreate, construct, reconstruct, assemble, compose, describe, organize, formulate, invent
Evaluation	judge, evaluate, determine, appraise, decide, compare, weigh, examine, calculate, critique

*Adapted from a chart prepared by the Field Services Division, Department of Pupil and Program Appraisal, Montgomery County Public Schools (Maryland), September 1973.

CHAPTER 3
THE RESEARCH RESULTS
OF THE PSR PROGRAM

INTRODUCTION

The Police/Student Relations Program is a delinquency prevention program designed to be administered by the public schools. Its rationale is that by teaching junior high school students technical information about law enforcement, student attitudes toward law enforcement officers will improve. Early evaluation indicated that the program of instruction, the PSR curriculum, did indeed change attitudes positively. The question remained as to whether the PSR curriculum subsequently changed the street behavior of students as well. If behavior change followed attitude change, then PSR could be considered a primary delinquency prevention program. One condition of the grant for the first year of the project (1974–75) was that court data on the experimental and control groups (Julius West Junior High and Broome Junior High School) be examined to determine if the program had made an impact on reducing the number of teenagers processed through the juvenile court. At the end of the first year when the data were collected and analyzed, the results were practically meaningless. There were too few cases for a valid study, and the accuracy of the court data was questioned.

During the second year of the project (1975–76), a second research study was designed. Its objective was to conduct an examination of arrest data of the experimental and control groups to determine whether or not exposure to the PSR curriculum in seventh grade could have an impact on the number of offenses committed during the eighth grade year.

RESULTS OF ATTITUDE STUDY

A major goal of the PSR program is to change the attitude of adolescents toward law enforcement officers and subsequently to influence the behavior of these young people. A noted sociologist has stated, "Lack of respect for the police presumably leads to lack of respect for the law . . . [the student] is free to violate the law if it appears that it would be to his advantage to do so."[1]

The first step in evaluating the PSR program in relation to this major goal was to determine if attitudes of youth toward police and the law could in fact be positively changed by their exposure to the PSR curriculum. The attitude study was designed to answer the following questions:

1. Does exposure to the PSR curriculum change the attitude of adolescents toward the police, the law, and the courts?
2. Do boys react differently from girls?
3. Does the length of time during which students have been exposed to the curriculum influence the results?

Additionally, extensive work was done on the test instruments in order to evaluate and refine them for use in future studies.

The results of the attitude study showed that—

1. The PSR curriculum caused a statistically significant positive attitude change in seventh graders toward police officers.
2. There were no significant differences between change of attitudes of girls and boys.
3. Time exposure to the curriculum was not a factor in changing attitudes.
4. There was an emergence of a refined and valid instrument for further research of student attitudes toward police.[2]

The next step in the evaluation of the impact of the PSR instructional program on juveniles was to determine if the positive attitude change evoked a decrease in the number of offenses committed by these same young people. With the assistance of a statistician, the staff designed a research study based on arrest data to determine the impact of the PSR program on juvenile delinquency. The questions to be answered by this study were as follows:

1. Would there be a significant decrease between the offense rate among juveniles who received instruction in the PSR curriculum and a comparable group of students who did not receive PSR instruction?

2. Would there be a significant decrease in the offense rate between those students who received instruction in the PSR curriculum *and* had committed an offense(s) before exposure to PSR and a comparable group of students who did not receive the PSR instruction but had also committed offenses before the time the PSR program was delivered?

3. Would there be a significant decrease in the offense rate between students who received instruction in PSR and had *never* committed an offense prior to receiving instruction and a comparable group of students who did not receive PSR instruction and had *not* committed an offense prior to the time the program was administered?

The results of this study are discussed in a subsequent section of this chapter.

BACKGROUND

On January 29, 1976, the Montgomery County Public Schools (MCPS) Council on Instruction approved piloting of three units of the PSR law enforcement curriculum materials. In keeping with MCPS policy, the council stipulated that the new curriculum could be piloted in a maximum of ten junior high schools. Social studies resource teachers in the thirty-two junior high schools were notified and directed to send their requests to be considered as pilot schools to the Department of Curriculum and Instruction. The first ten to apply were selected, and the sample population was chosen from these ten schools. Four of the original ten schools were not acceptable for the sample population in the research program for these reasons:

1. The PSR instruction was not taught during the time period specified for the study (i.e., it was taught too early in the semester).

2. The PSR instruction was administered to a special class.
3. The PSR instruction was only partially used.
4. Eighth grade students were included in the instructional programs.

The six schools used for the experimental group were: Argyle, Edwin W. Broome, Benjamin Banneker, John T. Baker, Redland, and North Bethesda junior high schools. A total of 1,081 students who received the program in 1976 as seventh graders were identified as the treatment or experimental group. A control group of 1,034 seventh grade students in the 1975–76 school year was systematically selected from the following schools: Francis Scott Key, Gaithersburg, Julius West, Newport, Sligo, and Tilden junior high schools. The number of students from each school and the paired relationships of the control and experimental schools are presented in Table 1.

Table 1

EXPERIMENTAL/CONTROL SCHOOLS/MCPS JUNIOR HIGH SCHOOLS—1976

Experimental School	No.	Control School	No.
Banneker	301	Key	239
Baker	249	Gaithersburg	258
North Bethesda	201	Tilden	235
Redland	267	Newport	247
Argyle	54	Sligo	46
Broome	9	West	9

The control schools were matched to the experimental schools with a consideration of the following criteria:

1. The school had not administered the PSR curriculum.
2. The geographic location or proximity of the matched pairs of schools helped to insure equality of socioeconomic

levels, population densities, achievement levels and scholastic abilities of students, and student accessibility to potentially crime-seductive areas (i.e., shopping centers, parks, and recreation centers).

When a control school seventh grade included an excessive number of students, the table of random numbers was used to select an appropriate number of students for the study.

It was not practical or feasible to randomly sample schools for this study; however, even with this limitation it is unlikely that there is an appreciable difference between the experimental schools and other Montgomery County schools in terms of certain crucial variables—socioeconomic level, scholastic ability and achievement levels of students, sex, and geographic representation.

TREATMENT

The PSR curriculum was taught by thirteen teachers in the six experimental schools from May 1 to June 17, 1976. Classes were distributed throughout the school day. In each school the social studies resource teacher chose the length of time the curriculum was to be administered. The time groups are presented in Table 2.

Table 2

LENGTH OF TIME PSR PROGRAM ADMINISTERED IN
EXPERIMENTAL SCHOOLS—MAY 1 TO JUNE 17, 1976

Time	School
Short (2 weeks)	Redland North Bethesda
Intermediate (4–5 weeks)	Baker Banneker
Long (7–9 weeks)	Argyle Broome

The previous evaluation of PSR (Attitude Study, 1975–76) had indicated that the time of exposure to the curriculum (from two to nine weeks) did not influence student attitude change (i.e., the attitude of seventh graders toward police improved significantly due to the PSR curriculum regardless of the length of time each class was exposed to the program). The next research was designed to see if there was a concomitant behavior change during the eighth grade school year among those students who experienced a positive attitude change as a result of the PSR curriculum in seventh grade. Two types of data were analyzed:

1. Students who had committed offenses prior to the exposure to the treatment (i.e., any offense committed prior to the date in May 1976 when instruction was begun)

2. Students who had *not* committed offenses prior to treatment (i.e., any offense committed after June 17, 1976, and up to June 30, 1977)

Any offense committed by members of either group during the weeks the curriculum was being taught (May 1 to June 17, 1976) was not included in the study.

The post-data collection was completed one year after the treatment was administered. Since eighth grade is the first peak in delinquency, the research was designed to study the impact of the seventh grade PSR program on offense rates during the eighth grade year. Permission was received from the Montgomery County Department of Police to examine the arrest reports on file at the Juvenile Section in the Wheaton-Glenmont Police Station. The evaluator examined the files for reports involving any students in the experimental or control groups. After the data were retrieved from the files, all names were eliminated to insure confidentiality.

RESEARCH DESIGN

A widely used quasi-experimental research design was chosen for the study—the nonequivalent control group design which requires an experimental and control group with both pre- and post-data. Although the groups did not have pre-experimental sampling equivalence, they were matched systematically. Their similarity was confirmed by the delinquent offense rate of each group prior to the time of treatment (Table 3). The analyses were completed with the use of the Z test between independent proportions.

RESEARCH RESULTS[3]

Predicted Outcome #1: *There will be a significant decrease in the post-offense rate for those students exposed to the PSR curriculum when compared to the students in the control group.*

The post-offense rate of the students exposed to the PSR curriculum decreased significantly ($p<.01$) when compared to the increased post-offense rate of the control group (Table 3).

Table 3

POST-OFFENSE RATE: EXPERIMENTAL AND CONTROL GROUPS

Group	Pre-Curriculum Offense Rate	Post-Curriculum Offense Rate	Proportion
Experimental	28	21	.0194
Control	29	56	.0541

$Z = 3.06$ $p<.01$

Predicted Outcome #2: *There will be a significant decrease in the number of post-offenders in the experimental group who had committed an offense prior to instruction in the PSR curriculum when compared to the control group.*

The number of students who committed an offense after receiving instruction in the seventh grade PSR program and who had committed an offense *prior* to instruction decreased significantly ($p<.025$) when compared to students in the control group (Table 4).

Table 4

POST-OFFENDER RATE/PRIOR-OFFENDER RATE: EXPERIMENTAL AND CONTROL GROUPS

Group	Pre-Curriculum Offender Rate	Post-Curriculum Offender Rate	Proportion
Experimental	22	2	.9091
Control	28	10	.6429

$Z = 2.189$ $p < .025$

Predicted Outcome #3: *There will be a significant decrease in the number of students who committed offenses after receiving instruction in the PSR curriculum and who had never committed an offense prior to instruction when compared to the control group.*

The Z test for significant difference did *not* produce a statistically significant result for this portion of the study. There was, however, a decrease in the number of students committing an offense for the first time for those who had received instruction compared to those in the control group (Table 5).

Table 5

POST-OFFENDER RATE/NO PRIOR OFFENSE: EXPERIMENTAL AND CONTROL GROUPS

Group	Pre-Offender Rate	Post-Offender Rate	Proportion
Experimental	0	15	.0142
Control	0	21	.0209

$Z = 1.175$ $p < .05$

DISCUSSION

The data analysis showed that the *PSR curriculum significantly decreased the offense rate of the experimental group.* This means that the PSR program can be considered a primary prevention program. The implication is that behavior change does indeed follow attitude change.

The second and third questions for the research study were designed to determine which *types* of juveniles were affected by the program. The two types of students studied were:

1. Those who had already had experience with the juvenile justice system prior to treatment
2. Those who had *not* had contact with the juvenile justice system prior to treatment but did commit an offense during their eighth grade year in school.

The results, which are critical, showed that the overall offense rate was affected but there was not a statistically *significant* difference between the rate of number of offenders in the experimental and control groups of those students who had *not* had any experience with the juvenile justice system before exposure to the PSR instruction. The results indicated then that the students whose behavior was significantly changed to the point that the offender rate was reduced were among *those students who had had a previous "brush" with the juvenile justice system prior to instruction.* The project staff predicted intuitively that the program would probably not be effective in reaching students who had already begun a pattern of offenses but would impact on those who might be on the verge of committing an offense. The results showed that the program impact was the reverse of what was predicted—with serious implications for educational programming.

In deciding to provide all seventh graders with six weeks of the law enforcement curriculum, MCPS was anticipating that a prevention program which reached seventh graders would be effective in reducing the eighth grade peak in the delinquency offense rate. On the basis of the study results, the real effectiveness of the program would appear to be its availability to those students who have had one or more brushes with the juvenile justice system. Since for each year of junior high school a different subset of students finds itself in that category, this means that the instructional program should be offered for two weeks in each of the junior high school years instead of for six weeks in the seventh grade (Table 6).

Table 6
Proposed Educational Programming/Delinquency Patterns

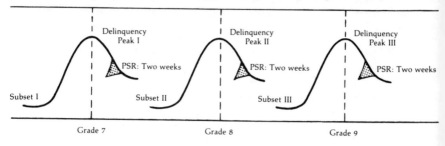

RECOMMENDED RESEARCH

The purpose of the study was to determine the impact of a school-administered program on delinquency rates. This particular study answered broad, general questions as to program impact; at the same time, it raised many more questions as to the exact nature of the changes which occurred. Some of these questions are considered here and are recommended for additional research.

Why does the PSR instructional program change the attitudes of students toward law enforcement officers? What are the dynamics of that change? Does the program change the attitudes of police officers toward juveniles? How and why?

If the criteria for changing attitudes through the use of an instructional program were understood, then other programs applied to other problem areas faced by the criminal and juvenile justice systems could be approached using the same principles. For example, groups of professionals who work within the justice system and who do not work together efficiently or cooperatively might benefit from training programs which provide each group with information about the others.

On what types of juvenile offenders does the PSR program impact and why?

The results now indicate that such a program changes the behavior of those students who have already had some contact with the juvenile justice system. Further analysis is needed to determine whether all students who have been in contact with the juvenile justice system are changed, or only those with simple offenses, and/or a minimal number of offenses. Or, does the program reach those who have set out on a pattern of delinquency and who, through some new understanding or appreciation of the system, have decided to meet their needs in some other way? If the latter case is true, then the PSR program should be implemented in juvenile detention centers *immediately.*

Does the PSR program have any impact on those students who receive instruction but have as yet had no involvement with the juvenile justice system?

There may be a time factor involved, that is, the impact of the program may occur only two or three years later or when the juvenile becomes an adult. Or, because of the program the student may commit only minor offenses, or there may not be as many students who after committing one offense go on to commit many more (i.e., the program may not reduce the number of first offenders, but it may prevent such individuals from becoming multiple offenders).

Is the program effective in other areas of Montgomery County and in other jurisdictions with vastly different population characteristics?

The research should be replicated with design improvements. The sample selection should be constructed to determine whether or not—

1. The results apply to Montgomery County generally.
2. Montgomery County represents a unique event in terms of program impact, or the same results are achievable in urban/inner city and/or rural areas.

Further, the study could be improved by randomly selecting classes as opposed to randomly selecting schools.

LIMITATIONS OF THE STUDY

The research results reported apply to those schools within Montgomery County which participated in the study. They are not generalizable to Montgomery County, nor can these results be said to apply to other jurisdictions. A broad-based study with a different sample would be necessary in order to make such critical generalizations.

CHAPTER 4
HOW TO START A PSR PROGRAM
IN YOUR JURISDICTION

This chapter offers the benefit of the experience of the designers and implementers of the original program in Montgomery County, Maryland. The experience in Montgomery County is not necessarily a typical one, but, taken with the duplication of the program in other Maryland counties, the warnings and suggestions made here may be applicable to almost any jurisdiction in the country.

SUGGESTIONS AND WARNINGS

FOR SCHOOL EMPLOYEES

If you work within a school system and are considering trying the PSR program, certain factors should be taken into account. First, this program is one of delinquency prevention through curriculum. With this dual label it often turns out that neither the curriculum department nor the pupil personnel workers (guidance department) view the project as belonging in their bailiwick. Your first task, then, is to convince the curriculum personnel that the instructional materials belong in their domain. You may wish to gather support from pupil personnel workers, counselors, or guidance personnel before approaching the curriculum department. These two departments are keys to the success of the project.

The size of the school system may determine your approach. If the system is relatively small, it may be appropriate to start with the superintendent of schools. At some point in time you will have to appear before the board of education with your ideas. In the Montgomery County Public Schools, a Council on Instruction is required to review and approve any new curriculum before it is inserted into the official school program. The council is composed of representatives from all levels of the school system including students.

Whenever you present the program to a group of persons whose support you would like to elicit, an order of presentation is recommended. Since the most difficult task is defining the program to the audience, this can be done very quickly if you begin by showing a slide/tape of a highly technical nature such as *Felony Stops* or *Narcotics Investigator*. Such a showing establishes immediately that you wish to teach law enforcement *not* police human relations or public relations issues. Some persons may ask: "Why are you teaching *that* to junior high school students?" Please read chapter 2 and be superprepared to answer that question. You will also need to describe both the attitude change and the offense rate change which occur as a result of receiving instruction in law enforcement as outlined by the program guide (both of which are discussed in chapter 3).

A second warning—in every group of people who hear about the program for the first time there is always someone who says, "But aren't you making better criminals?" The answer to that charge is a resounding NO for these reasons: The usual reaction by students is "Wow! I didn't know the police could do that!" Furthermore, it should be noted that *most* students are oriented to mentally healthy behavior rather than to deviant behavior. Therefore, most respond with respect for the professionalism of the law enforcement officer. The few students who may be heading for delinquency may either be deterred (see research results in chapter 3) or may commit the same acts anyway. Television and films offer far more ideas on how to commit a crime and get away with it than the PSR program ever imagined. Information on committing a crime and getting away with it is not included in the program. On the contrary, in an arson investigation, for example, students are taught how to search for and consider evidence to determine whether or not arson has been committed as opposed to a natural fire; they are not taught how to build an incendiary device.

A last strong argument for this program of instruction is that the subject area and exciting presentation techniques tend to regenerate student interest in school. This is particularly applicable to the average student—average in motivation, not in ability levels. For that reason many teachers in Montgomery County choose to teach law enforcement the last few weeks of school as a means of maintaining attendance and participation. It should also be noted that the PSR course frequently motivates students who have experienced considerable academic failure. Many of the skills required are those from which these students can benefit greatly. Radio communications, for example, reinforces listening skills.

The cost of the program will always be an issue within the school system. Several approaches are possible here. The initial cost of a packet of materials is minimal. Once the purchase has been made, you can continue by producing your own materials with the local police department. An alternative is to solicit funds from local organizations concerned with crime prevention such as the Kiwanis Club, or the League of Women Voters. As a last resort you may wish to appeal to the police department, a government agency, or citizens' groups. In such appeals your first concern should be a clear explanation of the program concept. Once citizens understand the concept and the program results, support is immediate. Most people today are well aware of the kinds of delinquency problems prevalent in their communities.

When you approach the police department for support to the local schools, it is important to be clear about certain points.

1. This delinquency prevention program is far more effective and economically feasible for them than almost any other. Many programs require many man-hours from the police department. Time requirements of PSR are minimal since the burden of instruction is borne by the teachers.

2. Some police departments may shy away with the response "We cannot give away our secrets." This attitude is a difficult and almost insurmountable obstacle. Again, it is recommended that you show materials immediately; secondly, have them read the research results; then try to convince them that the program is most flattering to the police officer. Invariably when an officer finishes working

with a group of adolescents under the instructional circumstances of the program, he/she is far more comfortable in dealing with the same students on the street.

FOR POLICE EMPLOYEES

The key person for police employees to contact is the chief of police, since the cooperation of this official is essential to the success of the PSR program. In Montgomery County police officers were first notified of the program by a memorandum from headquarters which gave descriptive background information.

When police personnel are initiating the action, it is important to stress the fact that the main responsibility for instruction is the school's. Consequently, contact should also be made with the chairpersons of the curriculum department and/or social studies department to explain the goals and purposes of the program. School officials should be informed that sample instructional materials and course outlines are readily available. A commitment of support from the chief of police assures them of police involvement and cooperation.

COMMUNITY SUPPORT AND RESOURCES

Whether the department of police or the school system wishes to implement the PSR delinquency prevention program, community support is critical.

A few suggestions may be helpful to keep in mind.

1. Be certain to contact *all* police departments within your areas. If you are located in a city, there may also be state police who are available for visits to classes. If you are located in a small town where you may draw heavily upon the state police, remember that there may be a small sheriff's office within the town.

2. Be certain to obtain an organizational chart of the police department with which you are working. This chart will tell you of the various specialty departments and divisions you can draw upon. For example, almost every police department has a patrol division, a criminal investigation division, a juvenile division, and a training division.

3. Contact the training division of your local or state police department for both field trips to the training facility and to borrow any audiovisual materials they may have on hand.

4. Other agencies within the criminal justice system should be contacted for some interaction with students. Be careful not to spend too much time on the abstractions of the legal system. You run the risk of losing the interest of the average students, even though you may receive accolades from the achieving students.

A list of resources follows which the teacher or police officer may call upon to support the instructional program in law enforcement.

Parent Teachers Association
League of Women Voters
Kiwanis Club
Local citizen groups
Social service agencies
State's Attorney's Office
Public Defender's Office
Defense Attorneys
Correction facilities for adults
Detention facilities for juveniles
Juvenile Court
Adult Courts
Private Detectives
Security Guards—local commercial establishments
Arson Investigation Unit: Fire Department
Coroner's Office or Medical Examiner

Crime Laboratories—Chemists
Federal Law Enforcement Agencies: Federal Bureau of Investigation, Internal Revenue Service, Post Office Department, National Park Service, U.S. Forest Department, Department of Immigration and Naturalization, Alcohol, Tobacco and Firearms

Other specialty areas:

Police organizations within the department—Unions or Fraternal Order of Police Officers
Female Police Officers
Sketch Artist
Canine Officers
Polygraph Operator
Victims of crimes

Ask the public and school libraries to set aside a collection of books on the subject of law enforcement and to display them prominently. These books will then be easily identifiable by your students and will show the community and other teachers what is going on in your classroom that is innovative.

CHAPTER 5
WHAT KINDS OF PROBLEMS SHOULD THE TEACHER ANTICIPATE IN TEACHING THE PSR PROGRAM?

The following are some of the questions that teachers ask concerning the PSR program.

1. *What if the students act up, expressing negative comments about police or asking embarassing questions?*

Let the interaction take place. The police officer has had training in working with citizens and has experienced this type of reaction while on duty. The officer can be expected to deal with the issues raised by students.

2. *How do I make sure the officer will discuss things which are interesting to students—or will stay on the subject?*

You cannot totally control what the police officer will do, but you can make very clear the questions and subjects which are to be discussed. You might provide the officer ahead of time with a list of questions the students would like to have answered. Other suggestions are:

a. To appoint one or two students as information coordinators on the day the officer comes to class giving them the task of keeping the discussion on the subject, making sure the basic questions are covered, or
b. To develop basic questions with the class as a whole, assigning one question to each of several students, making it a particular student's responsibility to be sure that "his/her" question is asked.

In the case of an officer who is invited to class to demonstrate a technique for a special piece of equipment, such as the polygraph, it would be helpful if you provided the officer with some idea of what the students already know (e.g., vocabulary, the situations when the technique or equipment is used, etc.) and with a list of points and questions you want the officer to cover. If the polygraph is to be demonstrated, for example, you might want the officer to discuss the physical limitations on its use, to compare and contrast its use with that of the Psychological Stress Evaluator, or to explain the role of the polygraph expert in testifying in court.

3. *How often will I need to have a police officer in my classroom as a resource?*

Probably about once for each unit. In Montgomery County, the Department of Police is prepared to respond to requests and to arrange for officers to visit classrooms. The background information provided in the individual teacher's guides is quite complete. These guides anticipate and answer frequently asked questions (e.g., in the activity about the juvenile justice system, quotations from sections of the Maryland state laws relevant to juveniles are provided).

4. *Law enforcement is not my field. What if the students ask questions which I can't answer and for which I can't identify a reference to research the topic?*

Teachers and students can build a "Questions List" or "Questions Bulletin Board" and at some agreed upon time consolidate and forward such questions to the community relations office, or ask the officers who visit the class as resources to answer them.

5. *Some students have had experiences with other programs which have something of a moral purpose (such as the drug education program). How do I deal with student suspicions that the PSR course is "brainwashing"?*

First of all, please do not, *yourself,* add an "Officer Friendly" or a "You'd-better-behave-or-else" dimension to the materials. An effort has been made to make the materials informative and descriptive rather than moralistic. Please try to carry that tone through in the classroom. Secondly, as quickly as possible, have students *use* the materials, *do* the activities, and invite officers to class. The students' actual experiences will do more to dispel their suspicions than anything else.

6. *I've set aside two weeks for two PSR units this semester. After looking at the materials I find there are many more activities and materials than we can possibly use in that time. What should I do?*

In planning the work with PSR activities, you may want to—
   a. Choose those which aim at skills in which your students are in need of practice.
   b. Select the activities you consider most suitable, list them on a ditto, and have the students rank-order them from those they would most like to do to those they would least like to do.
   c. Identify those activities which have been designed for use as a learning center (i.e., for individuals or small groups without constant teacher supervision and full class participation), and have them available for different groups to choose from. Time could be provided for independent or group work with these activities.

NOTES

Chapter 1. A Description of the Police/Student Relations (PSR) Program, pp. 12-23.

[1] Fact Research, Inc., *Beyond the Mid-Million Mark*, Life, change and government in Montgomery County, Maryland. Prepared for the Office of the County Executive, Montgomery County, Maryland, April 1974, p. 15.

[2] Clarence M. Kelly, *Uniform Crime Reports for the United States* (Washington, D.C.: U.S. Department of Justice, Federal Bureau of Investigation, 1973), p. 34.

[3] Montgomery County, Maryland, *Department of Police 1974 Annual Report* (Rockville, Maryland, 1974), p. 26.

[4] Travis Hirschi, *Causes of Delinquency* (Berkeley and Los Angeles: University of California Press, 1969), p. 70.

[5] C. J. Flammang, *Police Juvenile Enforcement* (Springfield, Illinois: C. C. Thomas, 1972), p. 148.

[6] Robert Portune, *Changing Adolescent Attitudes Towards Police* (Cincinnati: W. H. Anderson Publishing Company, 1971), p. 12.

[7] Marcella R. Lawler, ed., *Strategies for Planned Curricular Innovation* (New York: Columbia University, Teacher's College Press, 1970).

Chapter 2. Why Does the PSR Program Work Where So Many Others Have Failed? pp. 24-36.

[1] Aurora Gallagher, ed., *Juvenile Delinquency: A Basic Manual for County Officials* Washington, D. C.: National Association of Counties Research Foundation, Criminal Justice Program, 1976).

Chapter 3. The Research Results of the PSR Program, pp. 37-48.

[1] Travis Hirschi, *Causes of Delinquency* (Berkeley and Los Angeles: University of California Press, 1969), p. 202.

[2] Montgomery County Public Schools, *The School as a Primary Prevention: The Impact of the MCPS Police/Student Relations Curriculum on Juvenile Offense Rates (Academic Year 1976-77)*, Research Report (Rockville, Maryland: Montgomery County Public Schools, 1977).

[3] *Ibid.*

APPENDIX

APPENDIX

SAMPLES AND EXCERPTS FROM PSR INSTRUCTIONAL MATERIALS

The items in this appendix are samples and/or excerpts from three types of instructional materials prepared by the PSR project staff:

1. *Curriculum Outlines*. These outlines have been prepared for each topic and/or day of instruction; they include objectives, content outline, a brief description of the learning strategy, the resources, and an indication of the type of assessment task to accompany each objective. Guide sheets facilitate the planning of instruction.

2. *Individual Teacher's Guides*. A comprehensive teacher's guide has been prepared. In addition, for each objective a separate teacher's guide is available which gives explicit, detailed instructions on how to conduct each learning activity and provides answers to all discussion questions.

3. *Student Activity Sheets*. All student materials have been prepared, from worksheets to assessment tasks.

Specifically included are the following materials:

Curriculum Outlines

Criminal Investigation: Physical Evidence
    Day 5: Fingerprints
        (with Guide Sheet and fingerprint form)
Criminal Investigation: Specific Crimes
    Day 1: Arson Investigation
    Day 2: Homicide Investigation
    Day 3: Truck Hijacking
    Day 4: Narcotics Investigation
    Day 5: Robbery/Burglary/Larceny
        (with student activity sheets and report form)

Individual Teacher's Guides

Fire Investigator
Line-Up
  (with Line-Up Procedure Card and student activity sheet)
The Legal Code for Persons 18 or Under
  (with transparency and student activity sheet)

Sample materials are included herein for two reasons: a) as a guide for those wishing to prepare their own instructional materials and b) to illustrate the level of technicality of the instruction. Since the instruction should be at a high technical level, this latter point is critical to the success of the program. Many law enforcement personnel have reviewed the materials developed by PSR and have declared that the instruction would be appropriate for their police academies. Many hours of research, consultations with police experts, and review by police personnel have resulted in the high quality of the PSR products and have contributed to the success of the program in changing student attitudes and behaviors.

In order to hasten the implementation of a similar instructional program in your jurisdiction, you may wish to purchase the PSR materials. Contact the Kemtec Educational Corporation, Post Office Box #57, Kensington, Maryland 20795, for a brochure describing the products and a price list. The original PSR products have been made available in two student workbooks and one teacher's manual at reasonable prices. Individual audiovisual products may be purchased as desired or as the budget allows. The availability of these low-cost workbooks and the teacher's guide will help you to implement your program rapidly and effectively, without requiring additional time to prepare adequate instructional materials.

Unit 2: Criminal Investigation: Physical Evidence
Day 5: Fingerprints

SUGGESTED PERFORMANCE OBJECTIVES	SUGGESTED CONTENT OUTLINE	SUGGESTED LEARNING ACTIVITIES	SUGGESTED RESOURCES	ASSESSMENT CRITERION
1. Students will be able to identify three major types of fingerprints.	Three major types of fingerprints: • loops • whorls • arches	*Identifying Fingerprints* Students will record other students' fingerprints and classify according to chart. *Identifying Inked Fingerprints* Students will classify specific prints on fingerprint cards.	Chart: *Basic Types of Fingerprints* Fingerprint Cards	(Tests that accompany curriculum)
2. Students will be able to define terms which describe details of fingerprints.	Details of fingerprints: • ridges • bifurcation • delta • core	*Dactyloscopy* Students will complete worksheet on fingerprint terms.		
3. Students will be able to administer or take fingerprints on MCPD form.	Place correct fingers in appropriate ink substance a. Roll accurately on appropriate space on the form b. Fingers in, thumbs out	*Recording Fingerprints with Ink* Students will record inked fingerprints.	Filmloop: *How to Record Inked Fingerprints*	
4. Culminating Activity: Fingerprinting.	Lift latent prints. Identify suspect through class fingerprint file.	Students will set up a file of fingerprints, wash surfaces, plant prints, lift latent prints, identify suspect through fingerprint file.	File of fingerprints of members of class	

GUIDE SHEET

MATERIALS NEEDED

1. Chart of "Standard Types of Fingerprints"
2. Fingerprint Identification Cards from the Montgomery County Police, Rockville, Maryland, Bureau of Identification
3. Ink Pads

DIRECTIONS

1. Divide class into groups of three or four students each.
2. Pass out fingerprint identification cards.
3. Review process of fingerprinting as demonstrated in the filmloop.
4. Have members of each group take fingerprints of each other.
5. After all cards have been fingerprinted and all students have cleaned off their hands, have individual students identify their own types of fingerprints using the chart as a reference.
6. Direct students to select the three clearest prints on their own cards (placing a check mark under the prints selected).
7. Display the chart in a prominent place. Have students match their prints with the chart and write the type of fingerprints on a separate piece of paper.
8. Have students within each group exchange cards and identify each other's fingerprints.
9. Direct students in each group to compare their different identifications for each print:
   a. Does everyone agree on the types of fingerprints?
   b. What prints give difficulty?
   c. What are some confusing characteristics?
10. Display student fingerprint cards.

MONTGOMERY COUNTY POLICE, ROCKVILLE, MARYLAND
Bureau of Identification

NAME _____   CLASS _____

ALIAS _____

NO. _____ COLOR _____ SEX _____   REF. _____

RIGHT HAND

1. THUMB	2. INDEX FINGER	3. MIDDLE FINGER	4. RING FINGER	5. LITTLE FINGER

LEFT HAND

6. THUMB	7. INDEX FINGER	8. MIDDLE FINGER	9. RING FINGER	10. LITTLE FINGER

SIGNATURE OF OFFICIAL TAKING FINGERPRINTS	DATE FINGERPRINTED	SIGNATURE OF PERSON FINGERPRINTED

LEFT FOUR FINGERS TAKEN SIMULTANEOUSLY	LEFT THUMB	RIGHT THUMB	RIGHT FOUR FINGER TAKEN SIMULTANEOUSLY

DB #78

Unit 3: Criminal Investigation: Specific Crimes
Day 1: Arson Investigation

SUGGESTED PERFORMANCE OBJECTIVES	SUGGESTED CONTENT OUTLINE	SUGGESTED LEARNING ACTIVITIES	SUGGESTED RESOURCES	ASSESSMENT CRITERION
1. Students will be able to analyze fire scenes for evidence of arson.	Direction of fire spread Location of flames Odors Exterior openings and damage Unusual fire patterns Presence of inflammables, incendiary devices, other suspicious ignition articles	Students will examine slides for evidence of arson. Students will examine data and determine why or why not arson.	Slides: *Fire Marshal* Newspaper article: *Oneonta Daily*, "Feed Plant Damaged by Fire" Warehouse Fires	(Tests that accompany curriculum)
2. Students will be able to judge combustible on the basis of color of smoke and flame.	Magnesium Petroleum Butane Wood/Paper	Students will check answers against those concealed on wall chart. (To be added)	Wall Chart: *Burke's Procedures for Arson Investigation* (National Fire Protection Association)	
3. Students will be able to list motivations for arson.	Revenge Juvenile Destruction of documents Insurance	Students will brainstorm motives, then check results against those listed on chart. Students will examine fire investigator's notes and assign motive.	*Burke's Procedures for Arson Investigation* (NFPA)	

Day 2: Homicide Investigation

SUGGESTED PERFORMANCE OBJECTIVES	SUGGESTED CONTENT OUTLINE	SUGGESTED LEARNING ACTIVITIES	SUGGESTED RESOURCES	ASSESSMENT CRITERION

1. Students will be able to outline procedures to identify victim, motive, and suspect in a homicide.	Procedures to Identify Deceased
	A. Clothing and other articles
	  1. Traced by purchase
	  2. Jewelry
	  3. Personal possessions
	B. Whole body
	  1. Physical description
	  2. Fingerprints
	  3. Photos
	  4. Age
	  5. Teeth
		Students will proceed through clue cards for a homicide to outline means to identify victim, motive, and suspect.	Clue Cards	(Tests that accompany curriculum)

2. Students will be able to analyze data to determine time of victim's death.	A. Physiological Indicators
	  1. Temperature
	  2. Lividity
	  3. Rigor mortis
	  4. Putrefaction
	B. Life Style of Victim
	  1. Clothing
	  2. Routine
	  3. Companions
		Students will list questions that would guide an investigator in determining the time of death.	Transparencies: *Time of Death*
			1. Life Styles
			2. Time of Death, Physiological Signs	

3. Students will select procedures officer would follow in event of natural death, suicide, or homicide.	Consideration of Possible Homicide • Preserve scene of crime • Photograph, sketch scene • Search scene • Collect evidence • Examine body • Check victim's medical history	Students will view filmstrip and discuss decision made as choices are given. Students will prepare defense or prosecution based on evidence.	Filmstrip tape: *Homicide, Suicide or Natural Death?* Article: *Star News*	

Day 3: Truck Hijacking

SUGGESTED PERFORMANCE OBJECTIVES	SUGGESTED CONTENT OUTLINE	SUGGESTED LEARNING ACTIVITIES	SUGGESTED RESOURCES	ASSESSMENT CRITERION
1. Students will be able to describe the roles necessary in a truck hijacking.	Structure of Hijack Group 1. Fingerman — information on marked truck 2. Fence — receives merchandise 3. Spotter — locates, points out truck, follows in car, checks with headquarters to see if theft has been discovered	Students will identify character in audiotape who assumed each role.	Audiotape: *Truck Hijacking* Transparency	(Tests that accompany curriculum)
2. Students will be able to outline investigation of suspects.	Investigation of Driver: • Employment record • Police record • Associates • Associates' police records • Personal habits, living style • Trip ticket • Union • Usual and unusual stops	Students will construct questions (based on dossier) to ask driver of stolen vehicle.	Employment dossier on driver of stolen vehicle	
3. Students will be able to formulate the procedure to examine a recovered hijacked vehicle and the crime scene for physical evidence.	Exam of Vehicle and Scene: • Fingerprints • Shoe prints • Soil • Tire tracks • Used matches/ cigarette butts • Match booklets • Distance traveled	Students will examine slides of physical evidence for relationship to truck hijacking.	Slides / photographs of physical evidence	

Day 4: Narcotics Investigation

SUGGESTED PERFORMANCE OBJECTIVES	SUGGESTED CONTENT OUTLINE	SUGGESTED LEARNING ACTIVITES	SUGGESTED RESOURCES	ASSESSMENT CRITERION
1. Students will be able to judge which type of surveillance method to use for a given M.O. of a pusher.	Surveillance Method: • Foot • Auto • Wiretap • Telephoto lens • Fixed surveillance	(To be added)	Case Studies, M.O.'s of pushers	(Tests that accompany curriculum)
2. Students will be able to describe important factors for an undercover investigator.	Undercover: • Qualifications • Disguise • Contact with suspects • Maintaining contact • Procedures and pitfalls • Entrapment	(To be added)	Incidences: *Dave Morton* *FBI Law Enforcement Bulletin* Excerpts	
3. Students will be able to discriminate between right and wrong way to investigate.	1. Tasting narcotics 2. Removing evidence 3. Processing evidence	(To be added)	Slide/tape: *Rules of Narcotics Investigation*	
4. Students will be able to problem-solve to list places of concealment for narcotics.	1. Home 2. School 3. Auto	Students will divide into small groups and list places of concealment, then check their lists against transparencies.	Transparency: *Places of Concealment*	
5. Students will form an opinion as to ethics of undercover narcotics agent in high schools.	Means to infiltrate • Views of agent • Value to agent	Students will read article, form opinion, conclusions, and examine each one's opinion in relationship to other students.	Article: "Secrets of an Undercover Narcotics Agent"	

Day 5: Robbery/Burglary/Larceny

SUGGESTED PERFORMANCE OBJECTIVES	SUGGESTED CONTENT OUTLINE	SUGGESTED LEARNING ACTIVITIES	SUGGESTED RESOURCES	ASSESSMENT CRITERION
1. Students will be able to classify crimes as robbery, burglary, or larceny.	Types of Crimes 1. Robbery — taking something by force 2. Burglary — taking something without the presence of people 3. Larceny — taking something that belongs to another	Students will read or listen to accounts on flash cards of various types of crimes. Students will role-play incidents of police responding to calls of suspected felonies.	Transparency: *Types of Crimes* Flash Cards Police Call Cards	(Tests that accompany curriculum)

2. Students will be able to plan police pursuit of a bank robber.	Preparation for Police Pursuit
	A. Apprehension at the scene
	B. Immediate pursuit
	  1. Alarms / notifications
	  2. Roadblocks
		Students will listen to audiotape and outline pursuit procedures.	Audiotape of pursuit taken from E.O.C. records.
			
			(To be added)	

Worksheet: Using The Correct Report

Number of Questions Completed: _____

NAME: _____

DATE: _____

DIRECTIONS:
1. Read each incident.
2. Decide which of the three reports listed you would have to fill out if you were the investigating officer:
   a. Crime Against Person   b. Crime Against Property   c. Motor Vehicle Accident
3. Write the name of the report on the line after the incident.
4. Check your answers. If any of your answers are incorrect, fill in the correct answers.

INCIDENTS:

1. A citizen hit a hippopotamus which was hitchhiking on Route 495. _____

2. A citizen was clubbed with a zucchini squash, which was left at the scene. _____

3. A citizen was driving while intoxicated and drove two wheels of his car off a cliff. He escaped unharmed. _____

4. An apartment was burglarized. A moving van drove up; and two men, dressed as movers, proceeded to clear everything out of the apartment. _____

5. A citizen hit a fire hydrant which caused the flooding of a major intersection at rush hour. _____

6. A citizen's entire collection of shrunken heads was stolen while he was at the annual Medicine Men convention. _____

7. A chef at a famous restaurant was found poisoned. _____

8. One morning a rich citizen discovered that his gold Cadillac had been painted with yellow and purple stripes. _____

9. A citizen was driving along when her car was hit by a house being moved along the road by a truck. _____

10. A museum reported the theft of all its vases. The only clues were a rose and a note signed, "The Thorny Thief." _____

ANSWERS:

1. Motor Vehicle Accident
2. Crime Against Person
3. Motor Vehicle Accident
4. Crime Against Property
5. Motor Vehicle Accident

6. Crime Against Property
7. Crime Against Person
8. Crime Against Property
9. Motor Vehicle Accident
10. Crime Against Property

Worksheet: Report Writing

Questions Completed: _____

NAME: _____

DATE: _____

DIRECTIONS:

1. Read the accompanying story about a nighttime burglary.
2. Fill out the condensed version of the "Crime Against Property" report from the information given in the story. YOU are the investigating officer; so, sign *your* name at the bottom.
3. Check your answers with the already completed report. If any of your answers are incorrect, fill in the correct answers.

CRIME AGAINST PROPERTY	1. PERSON/FIRM FOR WHOM COMPLAINT WAS MADE (VICTIM)		2. RD. NUMBER
Montgomery County, Maryland **Department of Police**	3. ADDRESS	CITY - STATE - ZIP	4. CLASSIFICATION
18. VICTIM'S PLACE OF EMPLOYMENT OR SCHOOL (ADDRESS)	5. RACE - SEX - D.O.B.	6. PHONE RES.: BUS.:	7. CLASSIFICATION CHANGED TO:
19. VICTIM'S OCCUPATION 20. HRS. OF EMPLOY. 21. SOBRIETY	8. CRIME		9. P.R.A. NO.
22. DESCRIBE TYPE OF AREA OR PREMISES	10. LOCATION OF CRIME		
23. VEHICLE USED BY SUSPECTS LICENSE NO. STATE YEAR ☐ YES ☐ NO	11. WHEN OCCURRED MO — DA — YR MO — DA — YR TO HOURS DAY	12. WHEN REPORTED MO — DA — YR HOURS DAY	
YEAR MAKE BODY COLOR(S)	13. COMPLAINANT'S NAME (LAST, FIRST, MIDDLE)	14. RACE - SEX - AGE 15. RES. PHONE	
IDENTIFYING CHARACTERISTICS OF VEHICLE	16. COMPLAINANT'S ADDRESS CITY STATE ZIP	17. BUS. PHONE	

CODE: W—WITNESS: P—PARENT; G—GUARDIAN

24. NAME		CODE	RESIDENCE ADDRESS	CITY	STATE	ZIP	RES. PHONE	BUS. PHONE
25.								
26.								

27. IDENTIFY SUSPECTS BY NO. (NAME-ADDRESS-RACE-SEX-AGE-HEIGHT-WEIGHT-HAIR-EYES-COMPLEXION-CLOTHING)	WARRANT ON FILE	ARRESTED
(1)	☐ YES ☐ NO	☐ YES ☐ NO
(2)	WARRANT ON FILE ☐ YES ☐ NO	ARRESTED ☐ YES ☐ NO

28. WEAPON-TOOLS OR MEANS USED	29. METHOD USED TO COMMIT CRIME	30. ROUTE OF ESCAPE

31. PERSON NOTIFIED IN C.I.D. DATE TIME	32. TOTAL VALUE STOLEN $	33. TOTAL VALUE RECOVERED $	34. LATENT PRINTS ☐ YES ☐ NO PHOTOGRAPHS ☐ YES ☐ NO
35. TRADEMARKS OF SUSPECT(S) (ACTION OR CONVERSATION)			36. POINT OF ENTRY

WORTHLESS DOCUMENT	37. TYPE OF DOCUMENT	38. DATE OF DOCUMENT	39. DOCUMENT NO.	40. FIRM NAME OF CHECK	41. ACCOUNT NUMBER
	42. NAME OF BANK ADDRESS	43. MADE PAYABLE TO		44. SIGNATURE ON FACE	
	45. REASON NOT HONORED	46. TYPE OF PROPERTY OR SERVICE OBTAINED		47. AMOUNT OF DOCUMENT	

ITEM NO.	48. NARRATIVE: (1) CONTINUATION OF ABOVE ITEMS (INDICATE ITEM NUMBER AT LEFT; INCLUDE ADDITIONAL WITNESSES AND SUSPECTS); (2) DESCRIBE DETAILS OF INCIDENT, (3) DESCRIBE EVIDENCE AND PROPERTY DISPOSITION. (4) DESCRIBE PROPERTY TAKEN OR RECOVERED, ITS VALUE, AND IF RECOVERED CHECK THE **REC** BLOCK. (5) NOTE PROPERTY SLIP CONTROL NUMBER.	PROPERTY VALUE	REC	RECORDS USE ONLY T C

49. STATUS: ☐ OPEN	CLOSED BY: ☐ ARREST	☐ EXCEPTION	☐ UNFOUNDED
50. DISTRIBUTION EXTRA COPIES # DET. - PN - PE - PW - GA DST. - R - B - S - W/G INT. - JUV - SA - ME - FM OTHER _____	51. INVESTIGATING OFFICER NO. INVESTIGATING OFFICER NO.	52. DATE MO — DA — YR 54. REPORT REVIEW	53. APPROVED BY 55. RECORDS USE ONLY

M.C.P. FORM NO. 101

Peppy's Health Food Store

Pepper, John S.
100 Main Street
961-4270

791-3569

Bead Work
Macramé
M. Jenkins
Shop 791-7660

On Wednesday, July 2, 1975, John S. Pepper, owner and manager of Peppy's Health Food Store, was returning to his apartment above the shop at 100 Main Street, Rockville, Maryland (20854), around 11:00 P.M. (Police Time, 2300). A noisy, late-model, red Volkswagen van came speeding out of the back alley. Mr. Pepper entered his shop from the front. He noticed that the cash register was open. All the money, around six hundred dollars, was gone. Also missing were two cases of multiple vitamins, worth two hundred dollars, that had been stacked beside the cash register.

Mr. Pepper then went to the door leading to the alley. The lock had been jimmied, probably by the screwdriver lying on the ground. He reached for the screwdriver but decided not to pick it up. No other window or door had been tampered with. The burglars used this back door for coming and going.

John Pepper, a 34-year-old white man, looked around his neighborhood of small shops with apartments above them and wondered why *his* store had been

burglarized. Luckily no one was hurt. The only crime had been a nighttime burglary. It still didn't make sense.

His neighbor, Mrs. Mary Jenkins, of 102 Main Street, broke Pepper's train of thought by informing him that two men dressed in denim work clothes had taken a couple of cases out of the Health Food Store. The leader of the two was a white male, 6'2", 180 pounds, between 25 and 30 years old. He had long blond hair. Mrs. Jenkins did not get a good look at the other man. All she could remember was that he was a white man.

She told Pepper that she would be willing to share her information with the police. The police! Pepper dashed in and dialed 911.

YOU are patrolling that Main Street beat and Communications gives you the call to answer. After you arrive, you radio for the Identification Section which dusts for latent prints and takes photographs.

Based on all this information, YOU have to fill out a "Crime Against Property" report.

CRIME AGAINST PROPERTY

Montgomery County, Maryland
Department of Police

1. PERSON/FIRM FOR WHOM COMPLAINT WAS MADE (VICTIM)	2. RD. NUMBER
PERRY'S HEALTH FOOD STORE	

3. ADDRESS	CITY · STATE · ZIP	4. CLASSIFICATION
100 MAIN STREET ROCKVILLE, MD. 20854		

5A. VICTIM'S PLACE OF EMPLOYMENT OR SCHOOL (ADDRESS)	5. RACE · SEX · D.O.B.	6. PHONE	7. CLASSIFICATION CHANGED TO:
PERRY'S HEALTH FOOD STORE		RES: BUS.: 791-3569	

5B. VICTIM'S OCCUPATION	29. HRS. OF EMPLOY.	31. SORRIETY	8. CRIME	9. P.R.A. NO.
OWNER, MANAGER			NIGHTTIME Burglary	

10. DESCRIBE TYPE OF AREA OR PREMISES
SMALL SHOPS WITH APARTMENTS ABOVE THEM

16. LOCATION OF CRIME
100 MAIN STREET, ROCKVILLE MD.

23. VEHICLE USED BY SUSPECTS	LICENSE NO.	STATE	YEAR	11. WHEN OCCURRED				12. WHEN REPORTED			
☑ YES ☐ NO				MO—DA—YR 7/2/75 TO	HOURS 2300	DAY WED	MO—DA—YR 7/2/75	HOURS 2300	DAY WED

YEAR LATE MODEL	MAKE VOLKS-WAGEN	BODY VAN	COLOR(S) RED	13. COMPLAINANT'S NAME (LAST, FIRST, MIDDLE)	14. RACE · SEX · AGE	15. RES. PHONE
				PERRY, JOHN S.	W/M/34	961-4270

IDENTIFYING CHARACTERISTICS OF VEHICLE
NOISY CAR

16. COMPLAINANT'S ADDRESS	CITY	STATE	ZIP	17. BUS. PHONE
100 MAIN STREET, ROCKVILLE MD 20854				791-3569

CODE: W—WITNESS; P—PARENT; G—GUARDIAN

24. NAME	CODE	RESIDENCE ADDRESS	CITY	STATE	ZIP	RES. PHONE	BUS. PHONE
25. MRS. MARY JENKINS	W	102 MAIN STREET, ROCKVILLE MD 20854					791-7660
26.							

27. IDENTIFY SUSPECTS BY NO. (NAME-ADDRESS-RACE-SEX-AGE-HEIGHT-WEIGHT-HAIR-EYES-COMPLEXION-CLOTHING)

(1) W/M 6'2", 180, 25-30, LONG BLOND HAIR, WEARING DENIM CLOTHES

	WARRANT ON FILE	ARRESTED
	☐ YES ☐ NO	☐ YES ☐ NO

(2) W/M WEARING DENIM WORK CLOTHES

	WARRANT ON FILE	ARRESTED
	☐ YES ☐ NO	☐ YES ☐ NO

28. WEAPON-TOOLS OR MEANS USED	30. METHOD USED TO COMMIT CRIME	34. ROUTE OF ESCAPE
LOCK WAS OPENED WITH	BROKE INTO STORE OBTAINED MONEY +	BACK ALLEY
SCREWDRIVER	VITAMINS, FLED IN CAR	

31. PERSON NOTIFIED IN C.I.D.	DATE	TIME	32. TOTAL VALUE STOLEN	33. TOTAL VALUE RECOVERED	34.	LATENT PRINTS	
			$800	$		☑ YES ☐ NO	
					PHOTOGRAPHS	☑ YES ☐ NO

35. TRADEMARKS OF SUSPECT(S) (ACTION OR CONVERSATION)	36. POINT OF ENTRY
	BACK DOOR

<table>
<tr><td rowspan="5">WORTHLESS DOCUMENT</td><td>37. TYPE OF DOCUMENT</td><td>38. DATE OF DOCUMENT</td><td>39. DOCUMENT NO.</td><td>40. FIRM NAME OF CHECK</td><td colspan="2">41. ACCOUNT NUMBER</td></tr>
<tr><td>42. NAME OF BANK</td><td>ADDRESS</td><td>43. MADE PAYABLE TO</td><td colspan="3">44. SIGNATURE ON FACE</td></tr>
<tr><td colspan="2">45. REASON NOT HONORED</td><td colspan="2">46. TYPE OF PROPERTY OR SERVICE OBTAINED</td><td colspan="2">47. AMOUNT OF DOCUMENT</td></tr>
</table>

ITEM NO.	48. NARRATIVE: (1) CONTINUATION OF ABOVE ITEMS (INDICATE ITEM NUMBER AT LEFT; INCLUDE ADDITIONAL WITNESSES AND SUSPECTS); (2) DESCRIBE DETAILS OF INCIDENT, (3) DESCRIBE EVIDENCE AND PROPERTY DISPOSITION, (4) DESCRIBE PROPERTY TAKEN OR RECOVERED, ITS VALUE, AND IF RECOVERED CHECK THE REC BLOCK, (5) NOTE PROPERTY SLIP CONTROL NUMBER.	PROPERTY VALUE	REC	RECORDS USE ONLY
2	CASES MULTIPLE VITAMINS	$200		
	$600 CASH	$600		

49. STATUS: ☐ OPEN	CLOSED BY: ☐ ARREST	☐ EXCEPTION	☐ UNFOUNDED

50. DISTRIBUTION	51. INVESTIGATING OFFICER	NO.	52. DATE MO—DA—YR	53. APPROVED BY
EXTRA COPIES #	DST. · PN · FE · FW · GA DST. · R · B · G · W/G INT. · JUV · SA · ME · FM	(YOUR NAME)		
	OTHER	INVESTIGATING OFFICER NO.	54. REPORT REVIEW	55. RECORDS USE ONLY

M.C.P. FORM NO. 101

Worksheet: Motives For Arson

Questions Completed: _____

NAME: _____

DATE: _____

DIRECTIONS:

1. You need the following materials:
   a. Student Worksheet
   b. Burke's Procedural and Classification Chart of Arson Investigators
   c. Packet of Fire Investigator's Notes at the Scene.
2. Read each set of Fire Investigator's Notes.
3. Look at Burke's Chart and select type of motive.
4. Determine the prime suspect according to details given in each set of notes.
5. Complete the chart below by writing in the type of motive and suspect.
6. Check your answers. If any are incorrect, fill in the correct answers.

Note Card	Type of Motive	Prime Suspect
A		
B		
C		
D		
E		
F		

Answers

Note Card	Type of Motive	Prime Suspect
A	Household fire (gain fire)	Victim, owner of furniture
B	Automobile fire (gain fire)	Victim, owner of car
C	Juvenile fire	Seven teenage boys
D	Business fire (gain fire)	Owner of company
E	Fire to cover evidence of other crimes	Treasurer of company
F	Hate fire	Girl friend of victim

From Teacher's Guide: Fire Investigator

This activity is designed to help students understand that fires are considered a crime scene, and evidence can be collected to determine whether or not a fire was of suspicious origin.

DIRECTIONS

1. Present slide/tape on *Fire Investigator* to students.
2. Divide the class into three to four small groups.
3. Ask each group to assume they are the new Supervisor of Arson Investigation. Prepare a list of questions the Supervisor will use to interview firefighters after a fire to determine whether or not arson occurred. Each group may want to put its list on a chalkboard or newsprint to compare its questions with those of other groups.

SUGGESTED INTERVIEW QUESTIONS

1. What was the point of origin *or* where did the fire start?

   This is the first evidence to be gathered at the fire scene. At what point in the building did the fire start? This information may lead to the location of the incendiary device or other means to start a fire to establish that the fire was not accidental. Alligatoring helps to locate the point of origin.

2. What ignited the fire?

   This question leads to the search for evidence of incendiary devices—liquid accelerants or some other means to ignite a flame.

3. Were there multiple fires?

   Multiple fires indicate that an arsonist started fires at several places to ensure adequate ignition.

4. What was the direction of fire spread?

   The fire spread upward and outward. If the fire investigator finds the fire spread in a narrow or unusual pattern, it indicates that a liquid accelerant was used.

5. What method was required to extinguish flame?

   Sometimes when streams of water are used on fires, instead of the fire going out as might be expected under normal conditions, the fire will burn with increased intensity and perhaps with a different color flame such as red, blue, or orange. This reaction to water may indicate the presence of some flammable liquid.

6. Were there any unusual odors present when you arrived at the fire scene?

   Different flammables have distinct odors. Alcohol, kerosene, and other chemicals can be recognized. The fire investigator should familiarize her/himself with the odors of various flammable compounds.

7. What was the condition of windows and doors?

   By examining windows and doors the investigator can determine if tools were used to gain entry. In some instances doors and windows are purposefully locked and may be barred to prevent entry of firefighters.

OPTIONAL TASK

1. Have class read two newspaper articles, "Feed Plant Damaged by Fire" and "Mystery 3-Alarm Blaze Damages Interior of Warehouse in NE."
2. Have each group outline the investigation it would conduct of these suspicious fires.

From Teacher's Guide: Line-Up

The line-up videotape was filmed in the Metropolitan Police Department of Washington, D.C., whose line-up facilities are the most advanced in the entire nation. The Metropolitan Police Department uses this procedure more frequently in the process prosecuting cases than other police departments.

DIRECTIONS

1. Prepare the students to view the videotape by first discussing these questions:
   a. Why does the Detective Bureau use the line-up procedure?
      (To gain a positive identification of a suspect by a witness)
   b. What physical characteristics of the members of a line-up would you want to be certain were similar?
      (Height, build, type of clothing, skin tone, age)
2. View the videotape *Line-Up*.
3. Discuss the following points with the class:
   a. What procedures are used to protect the rights of the suspect?
      1) *(The suspect's attorney has an opportunity to review the line-up to be certain that all characteristics are closely matched. This ensures that the witness will not be clued as to which line-up person is the suspect)*
      2) *(The attorney may also state any objections to the line-up which cannot be easily changed for the record. When the case comes to court, s/he may be able to raise an objection to the line-up as a valid identification of a witness.)*
      3) *(Only one witness at a time may view the line-up so that witnesses do not influence each other's opinion.)*
   b. What procedures are followed to protect the witness?
      1) *(The witness views the suspect through a one-way vision mirror so that the suspect cannot see the person who may identify him/her positively as a suspect.)*
      2) *(The detective does not address the witness by name.)*
      3) *(The detective can turn off the microphone so that the suspect cannot hear the voice of the witness.)*
   c. In the *Line-Up* videotape what objections did the defense attorney have?
      1) *(He wanted it on record that his client was slightly shorter than other members of the line-up.)*
      2) *(He wanted his client to remove the 3 x 5 card and pen from his pocket.)*
   d. What requests did the witness have?
      1) *(To see a profile of the line-up members)*
      2) *(To hear the voice of each line-up member)*
   e. How did the orientation session of the witnesses by the detective help the witness?
      (The session made the witness less anxious since she would know ahead of time exactly what was going to happen. She didn't have to wonder.)
   f. Why is a line-up a tense situation?
      1) *(The lawyer for the person in a line-up is concerned that the line-up be conducted fairly to prevent any possibility of his/her client being identified by mistake.)*
      2) *(The suspect is worried about being positively identified, which means his/her court case will be more difficult.)*
      3) *(The detectives who conduct the line-up are concerned about the emotional state of the witness. In some cases, witnesses have fainted when seeing again the person who committed the crime.)*
      4) *(Often the witness is fearful that in some way the suspect will become aware that the witness is present and will retaliate on the spot. Also, a witness is experiencing fear of incorrectly identifying a person in a line-up or of not being able to recognize the suspect.)*

. Distribute Line-Up Procedure Cards to all students.
. Appoint one person to be the detective, one the defense attorney, three to be witnesses, and one the suspect.
. Have the detective plan and conduct the line-up.
. Have the class critique the detective's performance.

Line-Up Procedure Card

1. Match persons to participate in line-up as closely as possible. Check these characteristics:
   Hair (length, color, style)
   Height
   Build or weight
   Skin tone

2. Stand line-up members in a straight row.

3. Allow the defense attorney to review the line-up to request changes which would ensure fairness for his/her client, or to record minor characteristics which cannot be changed but might make the witness' identification of the suspect questionable in court.

4. Bring in one witness at a time.

5. Allow the witness time to look at the line-up members carefully and to request to see a profile or hear voices. (Remember, all members of a line-up must say the same thing.)

6. Say to the witness: *"Do you recognize any of the persons here?"*

7. Escort the witness to the door to leave without talking to other witnesses.

8. Announce the time and date of the line-up to be recorded.

Worksheet: Line-Up Procedures

Number of Questions Completed: _____

NAME: _____

DATE: _____

Line-Ups are conducted according to formal procedures.

DIRECTIONS:

1. View the videotape *Line-Up*.
2. Complete the worksheet.
3. Check your answers. Answers are at the end of the worksheet.
4. If any of your answers are incorrect, write in the correct ones.

QUESTIONS:

1. The line-up room in the videotape is the most famous one in the United States. In what city is it located?

_____

2. The suspect has certain rights protected. Who was present when the line-up was conducted to protect his rights?

_____

3. In the videotape what changes did the suspect's lawyer want to ensure that his client truly looked like everyone else in the line-up?

_____

4. The lawyer wanted one characteristic of the line-up to which he objected recorded for the record. What was that feature?

_____
_____

5. Certain procedures are followed to protect the witness. What are those procedures?

   a. _____

   b. _____

   c. _____

6. The witnesses are brought in one at a time. Why is this procedure followed?

_____
_____

7. The witness wanted to check two characteristics of the suspects. What did she request?

   a. _____

   b. _____

8. In the District of Columbia the entire line-up is audiotaped and videotaped. What does the detective say at the end to ensure proper identification of the line-up?

_____
_____

ANSWERS

1. Washington, D.C.
2. The suspect's lawyer
3. He asked that his client remove the 3 x 5 card and pen in his pocket
4. That his client was slightly shorter than the others
5. a. One-way vision mirror
   b. His/her name is not used
   c. The suspects cannot hear the witness' voice
6. To ensure that each witness' contribution is unbiased. So that each witness does not have an opportunity to hear the opinion of any other witness
7. a. A profile view of the suspect
   b. To hear the voice
8. Time and date of the line-up.

From Teacher's Guide: The Legal Code for Persons 18 or Under

This activity is designed to inform students of legal regulations that apply to their activities and behavior.

DIRECTIONS

1. Explain to students that they are a patrol division at the local police station. The station commander feels that there would be fewer offenses committed by persons 18 or under if such individuals were familiar with parts of the legal code which pertain to them. He has assigned your patrol division to prepare a student handbook.

2. Distribute the handout of the Legal Code for Persons 18 or Under, and place the transparency of the same title on the overhead projector.

3. Explain that the class will be divided into three groups to work together on the assignment. Each group will be assigned one category. Its task will be to research each item and to write a description of the law for that item. Tell the class they may add to the list but to be certain that any items added pertain to persons 18 or under and are not common law items relating to all persons (i.e., murder, arson, etc.).

4. Allow the class a few minutes to examine the handout and the transparency.

   NOTE: The three categories of legal regulations were selected to illustrate that some laws are enacted to *protect* the person under 18, while the motivation for other laws is to protect other persons from illegal or harmful acts committed by juveniles. A third category consists of regulations which are necessary to ensure the functioning of the broader community. The regulations placed in the center of the triangle which follows do not fit neatly into any category; they are regulations but not of the type that grant rights, privileges or responsibilities. Rather, implicit in these regulations is the protection of the following: persons under 18, community members, and property.

5. Provide students with some of the following resources to help them start on their research:
   a. Copy of Article 27 — Criminal Code of the State of Maryland
   b. Copy of *Juvenile Causes* which has legal requirements for Montgomery County, Maryland
   c. Assign one or two students to contact someone in the State's Attorney's Office to review findings for technical accuracy
   d. Assign one or two students to interview a lawyer for information.

OPTION #1

After the class has completed the handbook, request that the student government reproduce copies for all students. You may choose to invite a patrol officer to speak at the assembly at which the handbooks are distributed.

OPTION #2

If, in your opinion, the class has done a thorough job of preparing the handbook, you may wish to contact the Superintendent of Police, or the Community Affairs Office of the Police Department, to find out if they would like to reproduce the handbook for many persons under 18 in the community.

OPTION #3

You and your class may wish to include in your handbook one or more of the following:

A. A list of hotlines for persons under 18
B. A list of telephone numbers for relevant offices or divisions of the police department
C. Telephone numbers of other pertinent community resources and agencies (i.e., probation, juvenile court).

IST OF ITEMS TO BE COVERED IN HANDBOOK

. Laws to Protect the Person Under 18 from Harm

    A. Alcohol, consumption of
    B. Alcohol, purchase of
    C. Cigarettes, purchase of
    D. Drugs, use, possession, sale of
    E. Hitchhiking
    F. Restrictions on access to school and/or police records
    G. Runaways
    H. Truancy from school

. Laws to Protect Community Members and Their Property from Harm

    A. Assault and Battery
    B. Disorderly conduct
    C. Search of lockers on school property
    D. Search of persons on school property

. Laws to Regulate Community Activities for Organization and Welfare

    A. Compulsory school attendance
    B. Draft registration
    C. Driver's license, motor vehicle (auto, motorcycle)
    D. Learner's permit, motor vehicle (auto, motorcycle)
    E. Minibike regulations
    F. Voter registration

. Laws Which Regulate Behavior Which in and of Itself Is Not Harmful to the Person or Others but May Be

    A. Curfew
    B. Littering
    C. Loitering
    D. Trespassing

Categories of Legal Code for Persons 18 or Under

LAWS TO PROTECT
THE PERSON UNDER 18
FROM HARM

LAWS TO PROTECT COMMUNITY
MEMBERS AND THEIR PROPERTY
FROM HARM

Alcohol, consumption of
Alcohol, purchase of
Cigarettes, purchase of
Drugs, use of
Hitchhiking
Restrictions on
access to school
and/or police records
Runaways
Truancy from school

Assault and Battery
Disorderly Conduct
Search of lockers
on school property
Search of persons
on school property

Curfew
Littering
Loitering
Trespassing

Compulsory School Attendance
Draft Registration
Driver's License
Learner's Permit
Minibike Regulations
Voter Registration

LAWS TO REGULATE COMMUNITY
ACTIVITIES FOR ORGANIZATION
AND WELFARE

NOTE: Regulations in the center of the triangle are those which regulate activities because of potential harm either to the person under 18, to someone else, or to property.

Worksheet: Slide/Tape: Juvenile/Adult Arrest Procedures

NAME: _____

DATE: _____

DIRECTIONS:

1. View the slide/tape, *Juvenile versus Adult Arrest Procedures,* then answer the questions.

2. Check your answers. If any of your answers are incorrect, correct them.

QUESTIONS:

1. What was the charge for which the boys were arrested?

_____

2. George (age 16) and Arnold (age 19) were arrested at the same time for the same activity, yet at the police station they were treated differently. Why?

_____

3. List at least three ways in which George and Arnold received different treatment. (You do NOT need to find one way for each category.)

_____

	George	Arnold
At crime scene?	_____	_____
	_____	_____
At police station?	_____	_____
	_____	_____
By court procedures?	_____	_____
	_____	_____

_____

4. List at least three ways in which George and Arnold received the same treatment. (You do NOT need to find one way for each category.)

_____

	George	Arnold
At crime scene?	_____	_____
	_____	_____
At police station?	_____	_____
	_____	_____
By court procedures?	_____	_____
	_____	_____

_____

5. Which part of the procedures described in the slide/tape do you think constitutes an "arrest" technically?

_____

_____

6. Section 4-514 of the Annotated Code of Maryland, relevant to juveniles, is provided here.

   a. Read the quotation.
   b. Underline phrases for which you saw examples in the slide/tape.
   c. Write an example from the slide/tape for each phrase you underlined.

   "The Juvenile Act does not contemplate the punishment of children when they are found to be delinquent. The act contemplates an attempt to correct and rehabilitate. Emphasis is placed in the act upon the desirability of providing the necessary care and guidance in the child's own home and while the act recognizes that there will be cases where hospital care or commitment to a juvenile institution may be necessary, this is all directed to the rehabilitation of the child concerned rather than punishment for any delinquent conduct."

   _____

   _____

   _____

   _____

   _____

   _____

   _____

7. How is the practice of photographing and fingerprinting adults but not juveniles consistent with the goal of rehabilitating the juvenile?

   _____

   _____

8. In the slide/tape Arnold said that he would need to get a lawyer. George and his parents appeared at the Juvenile Court without a lawyer. Why was there a difference?

   _____

   _____

Answers

1. Damage to property.

2. George was a juvenile, Arnold was an adult.

3.

	George	Arnold
At crime scene:		
At police station:	Was not fingerprinted Was not photographed Released to parents' custody Parents were telephoned	Was fingerprinted Was photographed Released on his own recognizance Parents were not telephoned
By court procedures:	Received counseling from intake worker Did not go to a formal court hearing Did not receive a permanent police record Did receive permanent court record	Received no counseling Went to trial Received a permanent police record

4.

	George	Arnold
At crime scene:	Arrested Handcuffed Advised of rights Taken to police station	Arrested Handcuffed Advised of rights Taken to police station
At police station:	Again advised of rights Questioned further	Again advised of rights Questioned further
By court procedures:	Required to appear at court or court offices	Required to appear at court or court offices

5. "Arrest: An arrest is the apprehending or restraining of a person. It takes place whenever there is an actual seizing or touching of the body. An arrest may also consist of notification of the purpose to restrain an individual and his submission thereto." (*General Order Manual 72-27, Section Code 423-1,* Montgomery County Department of Police)

Other procedures which occur, such as reading the rights, follow the act of arrest.

6c. Examples:
1) George was not punished (by fine or jail sentence).
2) An attempt was made by the intake worker "to correct and rehabilitate" George.
3) An attempt was made to improve the "care and guidance in the child's own home" by the intake worker who had recommended informal probation and family counseling.

Part of the arrest procedure for adults includes fingerprinting and photographing of suspects with fingerprints and photographs placed in a police file. Juveniles are not fingerprinted and photographed. The court and police make every effort to ensure that a juvenile is not labelled a criminal. The assumption is that a juvenile will be treated and helped to adjust, whereas with an adult the attitude of criminal justice is almost the reverse (i.e., if the person has been charged with a crime, fingerprints and photographs should be recorded — it is highly likely he/she will commit another).

It is almost as if the criminal justice system views one offense of a juvenile as a symptom, a cry for help. Whereas one offense of an adult has a different significance: most often the adult has already made a decision to engage in criminal activities as a means of survival. (It should be noted that juveniles are fingerprinted and photographed when charged with a capital offense, i.e., one severe enough to demand the death penalty.)

The commissioner set a time for a trial for Arnold who had no choice but to go directly to trial for the alleged offense. George, on the other hand, was offered options. The first option shown in the slide/tape, was to meet with a court intake worker to review the case and decide whether or not a formal court hearing before a judge was needed. George was placed under supervision. If his subsequent behavior was not good, he would probably then have to go to trial.

In Montgomery County there is an interim step, not shown in the slide/tape. Between the arrest and the interview with the court intake worker, a juvenile and his/her parents would be asked to appear at the Juvenile Bureau of the Police Department to discuss what the juvenile had done and to assess his/her general attitude and situation. As a result of the information learned in this meeting, the Juvenile Bureau could decide to retain the case at the police station level, and not to send the juvenile and his/her parents on to the next level of an interview with a Juvenile Court intake worker.

BIBLIOGRAPHY

BIBLIOGRAPHY

BOOKS

Advisory Committee on the Police Function. *Standards Relating to the Urban Police Function,* Approved Draft, 1973. Chicago: American Bar Association Project on Standards for Criminal Justice, 1973.

Battle, Brendan P. and Weston, Paul B. *Arson.* 5th ed. New York: Arco Publishing Company, 1954.

Denfeld, Duane. *Streetwise Criminology.* Cambridge, Mass.: Schenkman Publishing Company, 1974.

Fatteh, Abdullah. *Handbook of Forensic Pathology.* Philadelphia: J. B. Lippincott Company, 1973.

Flammang, C. J. *Police Juvenile Enforcement.* Springfield, Ill.: C. C. Thomas, 1972.

_____. *The Police and the Underprotected Child.* Springfield, Ill.: C. C. Thomas, 1970.

Gallagher, Aurora, ed. *Juvenile Delinquency: A Basic Manual for County Officials.* Washington, D.C.: National Association of Counties Research Foundation, Criminal Justice Program, 1976.

Gerber, Samuel R. and Schroeder, Oliver Jr. *Criminal Investigation and Interrogation.* Cincinnati: W. H. Anderson Publishing Company, 1972.

Germann, A. C. et al. *Introduction to Law Enforcement and Criminal Justice.* Springfield, Ill.: C. C. Thomas, 1962, 1966, 1968, 1969, 1973.

Giallombardo, Rose, ed. *Juvenile Delinquency: A Book of Readings.* 2d ed. New York: John Wiley and Sons, 1972.

Harris, Richard N. *The Police Academy: An Inside View.* New York: John Wiley and Sons, 1973.

Hirschi, Travis. *Causes of Delinquency.* Berkeley and Los Angeles: University of California Press, 1969.

Khanna, J. L., ed. *New Treatment Approaches to Juvenile Delinquency.* Springfield, Ill.: C. C. Thomas, 1975.

Laurie, Peter. *Scotland Yard.* New York: Holt, Rinehart & Winston, 1970.

Lawler, Marcella R., ed. *Strategies for Planned Curricular Innovation.* New York: Columbia University, Teacher's College Press, 1970.

Moenssens, Andre A. *Fingerprint Techniques.* Radnor, Penna.: Chilton Book Company, 1971.

O'Connor, George W. and Vanderbosch, Charles G. *The Patrol Operation.* Gaithersburg, Md.: International Association of Chiefs of Police, 1967.

O'Hara, Charles E. *Fundamentals of Criminal Investigation.* Springfield, Ill.: C. C. Thomas, 1966, 1970, 1973.

Portune, Robert. *Changing Adolescent Attitudes Towards Police.* Cincinnati: W. H. Anderson Publishing Company, 1971.

Reiser, Martin. *Practical Psychology for Police Officers.* Springfield, Ill.: C. C. Thomas, 1973.

Rubinstein, Jonathan. *City Police.* New York: Farrar, Straus & Giroux, 1973.

OTHER PUBLICATIONS

Title	Publisher
Police Chief Magazine	International Association of Chiefs of Police Eleven Firstfield Road Gaithersburg, Maryland 20760
FBI Law Enforcement Bulletin	Federal Bureau of Investigation U. S. Department of Justice Washington, D. C. 20535
Journal of Forensic Sciences	American Academy of Forensic Sciences 11400 Rockville Pike Rockville, Maryland 20852
Journal of Police Science & Administration	Northwestern University School of Law and the International Association of Chiefs of Police Eleven Firstfield Road Gaithersburg, Maryland 20760
Fingerprint and Identification	Institute of Applied Science Syracuse, New York
Learning: The Magazine for Creative Teaching	Education Today Co., Inc. 530 University Avenue Palo Alto, California 94301
Harvard Educational Review	Harvard Educational Review Business Office Longfellow Hall 13 Appian Way Cambridge, Mass. 02138
Reference Services	National Criminal Justice Reference Service Law Enforcement Assistance Administration U. S. Department of Justice Washington, D. C. 20531
Legal Points	IACP Police Legal Center Research Division Gaithersburg, Maryland 20760

Title	Publisher
Crime and Delinquency Literature	National Council on Crime and Delinquency 411 Hackensack Avenue Hackensack, New Jersey 07601
Youth Alternatives	National Youth Alternatives Project 1830 Connecticut Avenue, N.W. Washington, D. C. 20009
Report on Education Research	Education News, Capital Publisher 2430 Pennsylvania Avenue, N.W. Washington, D.C. 20027
Social Sciences Education Consortium Newsletter	SSEC, Inc. 885 Broadway Boulder, Colorado 80302
More: Mediated Operational Research for Education	Project MORE George Peabody College for Teachers Box 318 Nashville, Tennessee 37203
ITYB: Intellectually Talented Youth Bulletin	ITYB Box 1360 The Johns Hopkins University Baltimore, Maryland 21218
Governor's Commission on Law Enforcement and Administration of Justice Newsletter	Governor's Commission on Law Enforcement and Administration of Justice Executive Plaza One Cockeysville, Maryland 21030
Youth Reporter	Department of Health, Education, and Welfare Office of Human Development Washington, D.C. 20201

SUPPLEMENTAL FILMS AND VIDEOTAPES

Unit Number	Title and Subject	Source
5	*American Crises: Crime in the Streets.* 60 min., 16mm, b & w film. (Delinquency and treatment)	Indiana University Audiovisual Center Bloomington, Indiana 47401
5	*The Great Store War.* 25 min., 16mm, color film. (Shoplifting)	NBC Educational Enterprises 30 Rockefeller Plaza New York, New York 10020
6	*Officer.* 20 min., videotape. (Search and Seizure Laws)	MCPD Office of Community Relations Programs 60 Courthouse Square Rockville, Maryland 20850
1	*Black Cop.* 20 min., 16mm, b&w film. (Human interest)	Indiana University Film Library, Indiana University Bloomington, Indiana 47401
1,6	*Perception of Danger.* 20 min., 16mm, color film. (Emotions and reactions to danger)	International Association of Chiefs of Police (IACP) Eleven Firstfield Road Gaithersburg, Maryland 20760
5	*Runaways.* 20 min., 16mm, color film. (Emphasizes emotions)	Little Red Filmhouse 119 South Kilkea Drive Los Angeles, California 90048
1	*Understanding Is A Two-Way Street.* 20 min., 16mm, color film. (Aspects of officer's job)	IACP Eleven Firstfield Road Gaithersburg, Maryland, 20760
1,6	*What's A Cop?* 20 min., 16mm, color film. (Incidents in an officer's day)	Motorola Teleprograms, Inc. 4825 North Scott Street Schiller Park, Illinois 60176
5	*The Theft.* 25 min., 16mm, color film. (Personal guidance, crime prevention, counseling)	Little Red Filmhouse 119 South Kilkea Drive Los Angeles, California 90048
5	*The Tunnel.* 25 min., 16mm, color film. (Gang violence)	Little Red Filmhouse 119 South Kilkea Drive Los Angeles California 90048